Befriending:
The American Samaritans

Befriending:
The American Samaritans

by

Monica Dickens

Edited, with Preface, Introduction, and Epilogue, by
Carlton Jackson

Bowling Green State University Popular Press
Bowling Green, OH 43403

Other books by Carlton Jackson:
Presidential Vetoes
The Great Lili
Zane Grey
J.I. Rodale: Apostle of Nonconformity
The Dreadful Month
Hounds of the Road
Who Will Take Our Children?
Hattie: The Life of Hattie McDaniel
A Social History of the Scotch-Irish
Picking Up the Tab: The Life and Movies of Martin Ritt

As co-author:
Foundations of Freedom
Challenge and Change
Two Centuries of Progress

As editor:
Zane Grey's *George Washington: Frontiersman*

Fiction:
Kentucky Outlaw Man:
A Novel Based on the Life of George Al Edwards

Library of Congress Cataloging-in-Publication Data
Dickens, Monica, 1915-
   Befriending : the American Samaritans / Monica Dickens ; edited, with
preface, introduction, and epilogue, by Carlton Jackson.
      p.   cm.
   Includes index.
   ISBN 0-87972-699-7 (clothbound). -- ISBN 0-87972-700-4 (pbk.)
   1. Samaritans (Organization) 2. Suicide--United States--Prevention.
3. Hotlines (Counseling)--United States. 4. Volunteer workers in mental
health--United States.   I. Jackson, Carlton.
II. Title
HV6548.U5D53   1996
362.2'87'0973--dc20   96-10815
                                                                     CIP

Cover design by Laura Darnell Dumm

Contents

Preface   *vii*

Introduction   *ix*

Befriending: The American Samaritans   1

Epilogue   115

Index   119

Preface

I was familiar with the books of Monica Dickens, with probably *The Happy Prisoner* as my favorite. When I read of her death in 1992, my first thought was regret and the second was that I would like to write her biography.

I got in touch with Mary Calvert, Monica's niece and literary executor, and asked her about the possibility of a biography. She was skeptical that I, as an American, would be able to capture the nuances of British life and manners as Monica Dickens described them in her books.

Of course, I objected. After all, Monica lived in the United States for thirty-four years. And I do have an English wife. And I did write a book about the wartime evacuations of British children.

But as I read and re-read some of Monica's books with this *nuance* thing in mind, I found that in large part Mary and my wife, Pat, may be right—although I am not going to yield totally on this matter. As an American, I probably never could fully understand why Monica Dickens, from a well-to-do, historic family, would go into domestic service. Or how there could be such comportment between those in service and those who were hiring. This is not really the "American" way of doing things.

Even so, I still harbor thoughts every now and then about one day being Monica Dickens's biographer. And I may have to move to England permanently to prepare myself—not an unpleasant thought at all.

Mary Calvert, I am glad to say, did not leave me empty-handed. She told me there was an unpublished manuscript in her possession that Monica had written in the 1970s about the founding of the Samaritans in America. Would I like to read it and perhaps fashion my own manuscript from it; or would I like to edit it. I quickly chose the latter, for I certainly would never fancy myself as improving on anything Monica Dickens wrote.

From May 1993 to April 1994, as a full teaching schedule at a busy university would permit, I edited Monica's manuscript, and wrote the introductory essay. It is a pleasure and a high privilege to be associated with the work of Monica Dickens. I thank Mary Calvert most sincerely for giving me the opportunity.

In the editing phase, I deleted several pages where Monica describes getting her drooping "Dickensian eyelids" repaired by a facial surgeon, because I thought it detracted from her anecdotal style of describing the Samaritans. Also, at various places, where Monica uses British spellings and terms, I have also tried to insert their American counterparts.

Certainly, I thank Mary Calvert and her husband, Brian, for their wonderful hospitality when I was in England in May 1993, as well as that of their daughter, Diana.

Here at my university, Western Kentucky, the faculty research committee granted enough funds for an airfare in May 1993 to go to England and study the Dickens material. I am grateful to each member of this committee.

History department chairman at WKU Richard Troutman, as always, was unfailing in his support and enthusiasm. I deeply appreciate his help and friendship over the years. My student assistant, Bobby O'Brien, helped greatly in this project as did department secretary Liz Jensen.

I take pleasure once more in thanking my family for their continued support: Beverly and Steve; Dan and Grace; Hilary, Matthew; and Colleen, Megan, and Katharine; and Travis, Patrick, and Austin. And, of course, Pat.

CARLTON JACKSON

Introduction

"I'm going to kill myself."

"What's wrong?"

"Everything. Everybody. Me."

"I want to help you. Please tell me what's happened."

"You wouldn't want to hear about it."

"Tell me about today. What happened today?"

"They had a meeting. I think it all came out. I'll lose my job, of course. I expected that. I'll lose everything."

"Your family?"

"I can't face what this will do to them."

"If you . . . how *would* you kill yourself?"

"Simple. I've got a gun."

"Where is it?"

"Here. On the table."

"Is anyone else there?"

"They've all gone for the weekend."

"Could you put the gun away . . . while we talk. Time. Give yourself some time. Put the gun where you can't see it."

"I'm scared."

"Don't be afraid. I'm here. You were right to call. You can't go through this alone. My name is Anne. What—no, of course not. We're not tracing your call. I understand. Tell me. You can say anything. It's all right to cry. It's safe. It's just you and me. I don't want you to die."

Thus—with this conversation that actually occurred—did best-selling British novelist, Monica Dickens, begin her 1978 manuscript dealing with the founding of the Samaritans in the United States.

The Samaritans started in England in 1953 when Anglican minister Chad Varah, opened a sex-therapy and depression-counseling service at his church, St. Stephen Walbrook, in London. Today, Varah's organization covers 140 countries, some with multiple chapters, 187 in the United States, including several in such highly populated states as New York and California.

Many times when visitors went to see Varah for counseling, they waited in an outer office. While they were there, the church staff frequently served tea, and the callers began to tell their stories. By the time they got to Varah, many had found their problems alleviated, if not solved altogether, simply by being allowed to talk uninterruptedly to the church staff, who did not see themselves as counselors, but merely as helpers who poured the tea and kept things tidy. Their nonjudgmental listening, which Varah dubbed "befriending," became "listening therapy," a practice that Varah turned into the chief principle of the Samaritans. Even decades after establishing the simple premise of listening, the rule is still "let the caller talk."

Primarily in America, and then mostly throughout the Bible Belt of the South, is the word "samaritan" given any religious connotations. In America, 'Samaritan' always derives from religion, primarily Christianity; elsewhere, this is not necessarily so. One who helps in the United States is a "good Samaritan," in the biblical sense of the phrase. In England according to Varah, "Samaritan" is not exclusively a religious term. A Samaritan is a benevolent person who provides material comforts. "You could get a great oaf of a lorry driver," Varah maintained, "clean shaven about three days ago," and when he meets the motorist who has run out of petrol he's apt to say "Well, I'll be the Samaritan." In Moslem and Buddhist countries, the word is simply not translatable. In Bahrain and Malaysia it comes out as "befriender" (hence, the organization throughout Asia known as Befrienders International), and in Sri Lanka, "Samaritan" is known as "Sumitro," or "spiritual companion."

Possibly Asia was the most difficult place to start Samaritan societies, because, generally, distressed people there tend to take their troubles to their families rather than outsiders. As Monica Dickens said, however, "tears need no translation," and "despair, anxiety, and loneliness know no geographical or political boundaries, and make no racial distinctions." As in Europe and the United States, when Asians in distress learned that the Samaritans were secular and nonjudgmental, and could be trusted, the organization began to flourish.

In fact, Varah, though the rector of St. Stephen and a canon at St. Paul's, never wore a clerical collar when dealing with the Samaritans. Moreover, not only the callers but the Samaritan volunteers as well could be of any religion or, for that matter, none at all. "Mostly I didn't know what religion they [the volunteers] had," Varah claimed. He remembered that "occasionally I discovered that someone would have a rather weird [religion], and then I would be a little suspicious as to whether they were trying to propagate it."

The first Christian Scientist, for example, whom he accepted as a volunteer presented no problem; but then two women professing to be Christian Scientists became volunteers, and they proselytized their faith, and were quickly told to "piss off."

At least in England the Samaritans did not run afoul of the medical profession (as they later did, in some instances, in America), who might have looked upon the volunteers as unprofessional competitors. The Reverend Varah suggested two reasons for cooperation from psychiatrists and psychologists. First was that medical practitioners constantly found themselves "tied up with somebody wanting to tell his or her life story at great length, when they had thirty or so other clients getting impatient in their waiting rooms. And they thought, My God, if the Samaritans can take these people off us so they don't bend my ear; jolly good."

Secondly, Varah gave many radio and television talks about the Samaritans, and continued to assure the medical community that the Samaritans were first and foremost committed to "listening therapy." They did not diagnose illnesses, let alone try to treat them. In fact, they frequently referred ill people to physicians, sometimes accompanying them to their offices, or surgeries. Thus, goodwill has always been a trademark between the Samaritans of England and that country's medical profession—so much so, in fact, that the staff at the Maudsley Hospital on Denmark Hill in London have been known to refer some of their troubled patients to Varah's group.

Though they did not seek to give medical advice, the early Samaritans still called their patrons "clients;" then they became "callers." "That is the fault of Americans," Varah says smilingly. "In 1953 a 'caller' was someone who came to see you. Then telephoning in America became 'calling,' and then we could use the term 'caller' as one who calls up rather than one who calls in."

Just what kind of people become volunteers for the Samaritans? Certainly class or personal wealth have nothing to do with it. In fact, one of the questions frequently asked of a would-be volunteer is "Are you ordinary enough to be a Samaritan?" Also, would-be Samaritans have to understand that their work as volunteers is taken from their own free time. Once they volunteer a certain amount of time, that time then belongs to the Samaritans, not to the individual. Not only must the volunteers be willing to part with their time and their families, they must also be prompt for their shifts of duty. Monica Dickens coined an apt phrase in this respect: "You're very late! Anybody would think you were paid!"

Each Samaritan is given a number; Dickens's in England was 1222; in the United States it was 12—because the United States was the twelfth country in the world to found a Samaritans branch. Last names are never used. If the callers were to know the last name of the volunteer, they might start telephoning homes, which would be unfair not only to the volunteer but to the caller as well. A caller might very well get an irritable person on the other end of the line such as a spouse or a child, and thus be worse off after making the call than before.

Inevitably, the Samaritans receive sexual calls. In her time as a Samaritan in England, these were the only ones Monica Dickens did not want to take (although she did, later, in the United States). Varah explained, "I suppose the only part of Samaritan work as I saw it which she was a bit dubious about was our willingness to listen to sexually demanding or sexually aggressive callers." Varah handled the problem by selecting a small number of volunteers who did not object to receiving such calls. They were all put under the generic name, "Brenda." "So whenever a person like Monica Dickens got that call she'd just say very politely, 'I'm sorry, I'm not trained to take the kind of call you want to make. Brenda isn't here at the moment. Just ring back at 3 and ask for Brenda.'"

Ultimately, Varah published a book about the Samaritan experience in England, and its incipient stage in the United States. He and his co-workers formulated several characteristics that were common to the suicidally minded. Among them were suicide as a solution to unbearable psychological pain, as a cessation of consciousness, and escape from emotions of helplessness and hopelessness. When he started the Samaritans there were three suicides a day in London. Behind the statistic were real human beings with real problems, though with an ambivalent attitude toward taking their own lives. The majority of those who killed themselves, Varah reported, had visited their physicians within three weeks of their death.

To do the best job possible with suicidally bent persons, Varah and his colleagues developed the "Seven Principles of the Samaritans" to guide their dealings with callers. First, the Samaritans were available at any hour of the day or night and their "listening therapy," it was hoped, would alleviate misery, loneliness, despair and depression. A caller never lost his or her independence by telephoning the Samaritans, even the decision to take one's own life, but in some instances, the Samaritan would invite the caller to seek professional guidance. The Samaritans were forbidden to impose their own convictions or to try to influence callers in regard to politics, philosophy or religion.

And, of course, the heart of the matter of all this was, does it work? Varah says, emphatically, yes! "I would never have started an organization to help suicidal people if I had been content to have been patted on the back for doing some unspecified good. I want to be judged by: did we or did we not prevent suicides?"

The statistics seemed to bear him out. England, from 1963—the point at which the Samaritans had ten years' experience behind them, with twenty-four branches—to 1983, there was a 25 percent drop in suicides. From 1973, in America, the year Monica Dickens started the Samaritans in Boston, the suicide rate—as she delineates in *Befriending*—precipitously declined.

Emile Durkheim's sociological study *Le Suicide* in 1897 asserted that suicide rates would go up during times of social revolution and chaos, and down in times of war. In the 1970s and 1980s, there were instances of both internal revolutions and wars. Yet, as Varah believes, the growing number of Samaritan volunteers helped immensely to bring down the suicide rate, at least in the western world, during both of these phenomena.

It is, as almost everyone in the field of suicidology knows, the spring that precipitates the greatest outbreak of suicide. "If you are alone, unloved, frustrated and depressed," Varah asserts, "and mocked by beautiful weather and mocked by the birds mating and singing and the animals mating and lovers strolling along in the sunshine, and everybody kissing and cuddling, except you, you go in that direction of possible suicide. It is," he added in understatement, a "depressing situation."

Wherever there are Samaritans, however, the rate has tended to go down. Finland traditionally has had the highest rates with 40 suicides out of every 100,000 of the population—primarily in the spring, and primarily for reasons cited above. Overall, Scandinavia is about 19 per 100,000. In England, in the 1980s, the rate dropped from 12 to 10 persons per 100,000 since the inception of the Samaritans. By 1985 the Samaritans in England were receiving two million calls a year. These averaged 6,000 calls every day or one every fifteen seconds. (It was not, however, just the western world that was benefiting from the Samaritans. During the 1970s, branches were founded, to good effect, in Burma, India, Pakistan, Rhodesia, Poland, Australia, New Zealand and Singapore), where suicide rates were apprehended to have dropped, though no statistical records are available.

Monica Dickens was best known in England not as a Samaritan but as a novelist. Conversely, she was known in the United States more as a Samaritan than as a writer.

She came from a family of one of the most highly respected writers in all the history of England: Charles Dickens was her great-grandfather.

Some of the older members of the family believed that no one should try to emulate Charles; that somehow the family's image would be tarnished if any other family member began to write. It was "quite a nerve" to contest the family's entrenched belief that there was and could be only one author named Dickens.

Monica Dickens attended St. Paul's Girls' School, in Hammersmith, and then a fashionable French school, was a debutante, and was expected to make a good marriage, but, like her famous ancestor, she had a personality of her own. Perhaps she inherited Charles's trait of being interested in, even fascinated by, people—particularly the down-and-outers—and trying to help them as much as she possibly could. Chad Varah explained: "She had no snobbery. She was, well you see . . . the English upper classes are not at all anxious about their status. They are invulnerable . . . blissfully unaware that they are archaic. They never care about 'What will people think?' It would be very lower middle class to worry about these things."

Indeed, Dickens reported that the waiters and the maids at the balls she attended were always "having a much better time than I was. . . . I wanted to belong to them, down there where there was a bit of life."

Thus, she went out and got a job as a cook. For the next couple of years she worked in several wealthy households, primarily in the London area, and learned firsthand what life was like "below stairs." She smiled inwardly whenever her employers, wanting to say something private in her presence, spoke French, because her knowledge of that language tended to be better than theirs. She would, however, never dream of telling them about it.

Nor, for a time, did she tell her parents and other members of her family, and some of her friends, that she had gone "into service." After all, she did come from the English upper middle class. Frequently at parties where she was working, she had to conceal herself from people she knew. "I had to hide behind a palm, or keep my head down as I cruised the crowd with my tray of Sidecars and White Ladies."

It was probably easier, however, for her relatives in England to accept that Dickens had gone into service than it would have been if they were an American family. There were (and are) nuances in the English class system that are not quite understood by most Americans. As Chad Varah said, the English elite have nothing left to prove. The English middle class, at least as it existed in Monica Dickens's day, saw nothing socially wrong with either mixing with or attending to the elite. She was just as much at ease catering to the elite as she was in joining them in a social occasion.

Most Americans would have been uncomfortable with this situation. Despite egalitarian claims, Americans are still quite class conscious. "He ought to remember his raising," will frequently be heard from an American about a friend or relative who has risen above the conditions of his birth. On the other hand, Americans tend to equate "class" with "wealth." If you have a lot of money, you have a great influence over economics and politics at all levels. Thus, you have "class." That is not quite the way these things are seen in England.

Class, in England, has more to do with tradition than the monetary wealth that is so often emphasized in America. In England, one can be from the highest class—because of history and inheritance patterns—and still be monetarily poorer than the middle class farmer or tradesman down the road. Yet, the farmer or tradesman would probably not be above joining the hoi-polloi in the public bar at the local pub while the landed gentry sat in the lounge.

Dickens was not "upper class" by birth. Her family were not of the nobility and owned no land. But her grandfather was a judge and her father a barrister, which put the family at the high end of the middle classes. Her grandmother was Lady Dickens only because her husband was knighted for his work as a judge. Monica Dickens, then, was "upper middle class" by birth; yet she was classless by disposition.

And this status greatly influenced Monica Dickens when she entered England's literary scene, at age twenty-two. She was at a ball on her night off when she met a young salesman who worked for a publisher. When he heard her story, he arranged for her to meet his employer—Michael Joseph. Monica Dickens told him she was "practically illiterate," despite her descent from Charles Dickens. Nevertheless, he told her to "imagine something very exciting, that's just happened," and write about it. Even so, according to reports, Joseph suggested that she might have to get a "ghost" to do the actual writing. She took this condescension as an "irresistible challenge." She began writing, but never quite got over the feeling that her literary career would never have occurred if it hadn't been for Charles Dickens in the first place. She knew that Charles was a good reporter, with an eye for detail, and that is what she tried to become. "All I have ever done," she said once, "is to report the experiences of my life."

Her first book was *One Pair of Hands*, about her life as a cook in the homes of various grand—and sometimes not-so-grand people— primarily in the London area. She wrote the book, in about three weeks, in pencil on a notebook bought from Woolworth's. It was, of course, primarily autobiographical, and it caused something of a scandal in the Dickens family. In fact, Lady Dickens, her grandmother, threatened to cancel her account at Harrods if the store did not discontinue its feature of *One Pair of Hands*. "Dickens was God," Monica Dickens said. "It was like someone coming along after Christ and saying they were Christ too." Her book became an overnight success, not only coming out as a bound volume but serialized in newspapers and magazines throughout the country as well.

Monica Dickens was now a writer, but when she finished her second book—a novel entitled *Mariana*—she decided to become a nurse. The literary effort that resulted from this experience was *One Pair of Feet*. It was a very funny book about the eccentricities of the medical profession, of how to outwit the senior nurse and stay out later than the usual curfew. One of the subjects it touched upon was death. Dickens described many instances of seeing people die. Foreshadowing her work as a Samaritan, she said that everyone young should see somebody die. "It's a helpful experience." She believed that death was proof that the essence, the spirit of the deceased, had "traveled on," and still existed somewhere. She wrote: "I haven't seen a light travel across the room but other nurses tell me that upon death they have seen a fuzzy light the size of a dandelion leave the body and travel outward and suddenly disappear," embarking on the next journey. Was this phenomenon their souls? Or was it merely the imagination of the attending nurses and doctors? Who is to say?

In addition to working in service just as World War II was breaking out, studying nursing and practicing it for a time during the war, Dickens also joined the war effort in other ways. For example, she worked for a time in a factory repairing Spitfires, and as a riveter in other aircraft plants. The book she wrote from her wartime factory experiences was *The Fancy*.

From 1946 to the end of the decade, Dickens was busy, averaging a book a year, including *The Happy Prisoner*, whose main character, Oliver North, discovered a number of important truths while recuperating from injuries received during the war. Other of her books from the mid to late 1940s were *Thursday Afternoons* (1945), *Joy and Josephine* (1948) and *Flowers in the Grass* (1945). Like Charles Dickens before her, she wrote with the eye of a reporter, noting the small details that convey the whole. She won praise from J.B. Priestley, who said, "Monica Dickens gets better and better." Rebecca West confirmed Priestley's opinion by asserting that "it is life itself that is caught up" in Monica Dickens's works.

She did actually become a reporter, working for a time for the *Hertfordshire Express*. The book derived from that experience was *My Turn to Make the Tea* (1951). There was a little bit of a joke contained in her title. Since she was the only woman reporter on the paper, as she said, it was *always* her turn to make the tea. "I have a great feeling for the bottom and background of things," she explained to a friend about her growing list of books that either depicted her own life's experiences or those of the "marginal characters" she met along the way. Even after she quit working for the weekly newspaper, she continued to write for a magazine entitled *Woman's Own*. She wrote her column for the next twenty years, even while producing some of her most memorable novels. She was discontinued by *Woman's Own* when a teen-ager from Liverpool wrote to the editor, demanding that someone younger than Monica Dickens be assigned to the column.

As a writer of some note, Dickens began to travel extensively. She visited the United States for the first time in 1946, coming over aboard a steamer, probably the *Mauritania*. In New York, she wrote in a diary, she wandered alone around the city, talking with numerous strangers (noting several years later that things changed dramatically in this respect). She was fascinated by an American football game she watched on a barroom television. Entranced by the marching bands and cheerleaders, she found the game to be not as rough, actually, as English rugby. The plays she saw included *A Streetcar Named Desire*, which she found "shattering," *Mr. Roberts,* and *Copacabana*.

On this trip she appeared in bookstores, autographing several of her recent works. She was, as might be expected, mistaken by numerous people as a *representative* of Charles Dickens, rather than a descendant and legitimate author in her own right. One patron walked into a bookstore and asked her please to sign a copy of *David Copperfield*. Still others thought she was descended from another famous English author: one person asked her, "Are you *really* William Shakespeare's granddaughter?"

She never did try, on any of these author engagements, to trade on her famous name. The only time she went out of her way to tell people she was descended from Charles Dickens was in the 1970s when she raised money to start the Samaritans in Boston, and she was not beyond impressing a few "fat cats."

On one of Dickens's flights in England, her seat partner was a Commander in the United States Navy. He was struggling over a diabolical English crossword puzzle, and she offered to help him with it. His name was Roy Olin Stratton, and he and Monica were married in 1951. She was thirty-five years old.

Roy came to England on numerous naval affairs in the immediate postwar period. Though he liked England, he loved Cape Cod; there was, quite plainly in his opinion, no other place on earth in which to make one's home. When Roy retired from the navy in 1953, Monica moved to Cape Cod with him, and lived there—still pursuing a literary career—for thirty-four years. She, too, was enamored of Cape Cod; yet she told a high school graduating class once not to let themselves be "trapped" by Cape Cod. Instead, they should go out and see some of the rest of the world before Cape Cod became an "island with no ferry to the mainland."

In Cape Cod, Monica Dickens Stratton flourished. If the door to her "writing room" was shut in daytime, that meant you couldn't go in. In one corner was a large built-in desk where she did her work. She would get up early in the morning and write for a couple of hours, before anybody else arose. Sometimes, however, she might cook for up to a dozen house guests, look after her stables, which always housed at least four horses, go on a trail ride, put a picnic together, take a swim, and be back at the house while everybody else just lazed around. She greeted everyone who came to see her and Roy at their North Falmouth home with "Hello, darling," and a warm hug, at once putting them at ease. She loved games, both active and passive. Even after a day of intense activity (according to several people), she would still be ready for a game of rounders (a form of English baseball), but then, once inside for the evening, there were games like Scrabble and Rummikub to be played at the kitchen table after supper.

According to her friends, her greatest gift, as a wife, mother, grandmother, sister, or aunt, was the ability to listen. "She never talked about herself," said one of her admirers, but she always listened to everyone else. And this is what made her such a good Samaritan.

Monica made regular visits back to England. She and Roy even bought a flat in Kensington, a part of London that Monica referred to as "the centre of the Universe." As she continued to write, with a new novel appearing every year or two, and to look for subjects to write about, it was not particularly inevitable, but perhaps predictable, that she come across the Samaritans.

That is what took her on that fateful day in 1969 to see the Reverend Chad Varah to interview him for a book she wanted to write about the effects of loneliness and depression. Of course she had heard about the Samaritans, and thought their experiences the best source for her work. The novel she wrote was titled *The Listeners* in England, but, because Taylor Caldwell had "stolen" the title in the United States, the book was known here as *The End of the Line*. In many ways it was a shattering novel, chronicling the misfortunes of several different people. In some instances, there was a happy ending; in others not. Monica Dickens wrote about these people in a nonjudgmental, nonsentimental way. Some were people born with proclivities toward suicide; others came to think of suicide because of traumatic incidents in their lives. Above all, as Dickens concluded in this and other books, those bent on suicide are not as interested in killing themselves as in wishing not to live. There is a great difference between those two points of view. All of the characters in this novel were based on real-life Samaritan callers, but Monica Dickens did not, of course, divulge any real identities. Though, generally, books about highly depressing subjects do not go over well, *The Listeners* in England and *The End of the Line* in the United States sold quite respectably, and received some good reviews.

Greater than the book she wrote was the personal transformation she went through with her continued interviews of Chad Varah It became increasingly clear to both Dickens and Varah that she certainly did not want just to stop with the book. She wanted to be a Samaritan.

"We took to one another very much," Chad Varah recalled. "I admired her writing as I did her grandfather's." After she came to Varah two or three times collecting material for her book on the Samaritans, it became obvious to Varah and also to Dickens that she was suited for and perhaps was meant to be, a Samaritan. She asked Varah if she could attend some of the Samaritan preparation classes. She knew that there was no way of becoming a Samaritan simply by payment of a fee or recommendation by a prominent individual. You would have to be someone who, at one end of the telephone—with a suicidal person at the other—would not complicate the matter. "And people who won't make the situation worse," mused Varah, "are rather rare."

To become a Samaritan, Dickens had to attend a series of seminars, lectures and discussions, on the subject of suicide. What causes people to contemplate taking their own lives? The problems are primarily related to sexuality, loneliness, marital situations, alcohol and drug addiction. (Later on, Monica Dickens would conduct several of these "learning sessions.")

A Samaritan volunteer must "relate constructively and encouragingly" to the person who either telephones or visits in person. The listening therapy involves no advice, no exhortation, no preaching, and definitely no making of a judgment. "This is what we call 'befriending,'" Varah says. In one way or another, he asserts, "we are all callers."

Dickens took the orientation lessons, and was not pleased with them. She thought she had failed the test. One of the volunteers pretended to be a caller, and the questions he asked left Dickens nonplused more than once. She did not, she believed, give the right nuance to the words she spoke to the person; she did not *listen* enough—

her inclination was to talk to the caller—and she did not, in her own mind, give the right kind of advice. Her cohorts in Varah's London office, however, disagreed with her assessment of the situation. They gave her an "overwhelming feeling of acceptance," saying that they had "all been there before . . . had been through it." Of Varah's group, Dickens later said it was the "first group I had ever been among where I think I could safely be myself." There was no putting on; an act to be what she thought people "might possibly want her to be." It was real, genuine and truthful, and therefore joyful.

Very quickly, Dickens picked up one characteristic of Samaritans everywhere: the ability to laugh in the midst of trauma. She learned that the "Eighth Principle" of the Samaritans was "Thou shalt not accept anyone among ourselves as a volunteer who does not have a sense of humor." Once a serious-minded minister of the gospel visited her Samaritan office and found everyone, including Monica Dickens, uproariously laughing. "But you're supposed to be involved in suicide," was his incredulous reaction. "Why, then, are you laughing so?" Monica's response became standard to this question: "If we don't laugh, we're sunk."

Important, too, was the quick sense of camaraderie that developed among the volunteers. They were all in the business of befriending for the "long haul;" even so, many were affected by the frequently sad nature of their calls. One of the volunteers Monica Dickens herself later recruited said that "one of the most important and wonderful things we had was if for any reason we were overwhelmed or immersed in feelings of undue sadness due to our work, we could always talk things out. In other words, we were never alone, but in it all together. In fact, that unity was our strength."

Another volunteer told how his life was changed by becoming a Samaritan. "Someone used to call regularly on my Sunday night shift," he reported, "and not say anything." The Samaritan would not hang up; he would put the phone down and check it from time to time to see if the caller wanted to talk, or had hung up.

"After many weeks of this had gone by, I was surprised when the silent caller said 'Hello.' It was an incredibly timid voice, like that of an injured bird. She at once hung up."

Weeks passed, and all the caller would say was "Hello." One night, though, she extended the conversation. "She was convinced that she had multiple personalities and could only call me when she was herself, the person who would talk to me."

As the Samaritan coaxed the caller, she divulged "tales of abuse by her father, some so severe that she had a crippled arm. I believed her to have multiple personality disorders and finally managed to convince her to see a psychologist friend of mine."

Showing how personally involved these Samaritan volunteers became in their work, this one, a male, "cried on the last night of my Samaritan service when I told her goodbye, as did she. This voice that was only connected to me by an assumed name and a telephone (and I never had her number—she only had mine) had become very much a part of my life." So much a part of his life, apparently, that he could write: "She sent me a small gift through the Samaritans and I was amazed. It was something that I had been asking my wife for years to get me and she never had. I don't think it was a coincidence. Somehow the woman behind the voice knew."

This volunteer stated the Samaritan experience "was of great importance to me in that it solidified my desire to become a social worker." He went to school and received a Master's Degree in Social Work, and today (mid 90s) works as a geriatric social worker. The Samaritan experience, it seems clear, has many byroads, and super-highways to turn off onto.

Monica Dickens continued to commute back and forth across the Atlantic, to research her books and publicize them, and also to work with Varah's befriending society. In the early 1970s, however, Monica and Roy sold their London apartment, and Monica thereafter began to spend almost all her time on Cape Cod, attending to her growing household. She and Roy had adopted two daughters, Pamela and Prudence, and for years Monica directed a house full of sleep-overs, arranged picnics at the beach, and tended to horses and dogs. She did not, however, neglect her writing during this period. She started a series of juvenile novels known as the Follyfoot series which were linked with a TV series based on one of her earlier novels, about a home for old horses. Among her other offerings in the 1970s were: *Talking of Horses,* her *World's End* children's series, *Last Year When I Was Young* (a novel), and *An Open Book,* (1978), her autobiography.

As the manuscript that follows relates, Monica Dickens was responsible for establishing the first branch of the Samaritans in the United States—in Boston. She was greatly encouraged in this endeavor by Chad Varah himself, who came frequently to visit Monica and Roy on the Cape—"in that beautiful house—at North Falmouth. Well, I was the one who told her she had to do it," Varah says. Dickens had told Varah that she would miss her Samaritan work now that she was no longer visiting London on a regular basis. "Nonsense," Varah said to her. "You are not going to miss working with the Samaritans, because you are going to start a branch in Massachusetts."

But the Americans, both Dickens and Varah surmised, were so *psychiatrically oriented.* Everybody had his own psychiatrist or psychologist, and would therefore pay little attention to someone who openly sponsored a befriending agency to benefit primarily the suicidal, but, in fact, anyone who had a problem he or she felt a need to talk to others about. Changing the word "befriending" to "counseling" helped to interest an increasing number of Americans in the movement. Despite her difficulties in getting the Boston branch started, as Dickens describes in this book, she never once telephoned Chad Varah to complain about the circumstances. She did, however, write to Varah quite frequently, and he in turn encouraged her to keep going forward. He pointed out to Monica that the United States was the twelfth country to start a branch of the Samaritans. Although her number in England had been 1222, in America, it needed to be changed. She therefore became known as "Monica 12."

It is seventy miles from Cape Cod to Boston, whichever route one follows. Each morning, rain, snow or shine, while the Boston branch was getting underway, Monica drove the distance in her beloved Saab (Roy had another one), and then she drove back in the evening. When Chad Varah was visiting, he went with her every day. He became a sort of sounding board. Even so, Varah said that "no credit attaches to me" for the way Monica Dickens created the Boston branch of the Samaritans. "I listened to her and I encouraged her and I asked questions which drew things out from her." But he could never remember ever giving Dickens any explicit advice. Her descriptions of forming the Boston branch of the Samaritans always ended with Varah telling her, "I think what you've decided is the best answer." The two, Monica Dickens and Chad Varah, were never at cross purposes with one another: "and we were good enough friends to be at cross purposes if we wanted and needed to be."

The Boston branch of the Samaritans, soon after its inception, began receiving more telephone calls than anyone in their wildest fantasies could ever have imagined. Certainly, the number of troubled individuals in "The Athens of America" was more than most people expected. Very quickly, Monica Dickens realized that people in Boston and people in London were not all that different from one another. In both places, the phrase, "I want to kill myself" almost always did not mean that "I want to be dead." Therefore, "listening therapy" in both cities, Boston and London, was of critical importance.

Very quickly, too, Dickens established the rule in Boston that the Samaritans were not there simply for the suicidal or for people in crisis.

The Samaritans were there for "anyone who needs someone to talk to in confidence at any time for any reason."

Even while she drove almost daily from Cape Cod to Boston to take care of the Samaritans, Monica Dickens continued to write and to take promotional tours for her books. One of her best anecdotes was about one of her Australian tours, when she spent a day in a bookstore signing her books. One woman bought a book and Dickens asked her name for the inscription. The woman answered "Emma Chiset," and Monica began to write "To Emma Chiset . . ." "No, no!" the woman replied firmly, "Emma Chiset?" She was, of course, asking the price of the book.

Finally, however, the trips to Boston became too much, even for the vivacious, effervescent Monica Dickens. As *Befriending* indicates, she began to feel she was neglecting her husband and daughters. She decided to put the Boston branch of the Samaritans into other hands and to spend more time on the Cape. The person who ultimately took charge of the Boston Samaritans was Marvin Ishai, who, at age fifty, had lived for many years in Israel, in a kibbutz in the Golan Heights.

Interestingly enough, after a few months in North Falmouth, Monica decided that the time had come to start a Samaritan branch on Cape Cod. Generally, the first reaction from everyone was, What? Start a Samaritan society here in the Utopia known as Cape Cod? But there were more than enough troubled people on Cape Cod to make her efforts realistic and worthwhile.

One of her projects was the erection of suicide barriers on the Bourne and Sagamore bridges across the Cape Cod canal leading to the mainland. She recounts in full in *Befriending,* how she and her colleagues went about getting the U.S. Corps of Engineers to put up the barriers. What she does not relate is that her efforts ultimately won praise for her and the Samaritans from Massachusetts Congressman Gary Studds. He put into the *Congressional Record* the following words, in celebration of the tenth anniversary of the Samaritans on Cape Cod:

Founded in 1977 by Monica Dickens Stratton, great-granddaughter of Charles Dickens, the Samaritan branch of Cape Cod is part of a world wide organization of volunteers committed to preventing suicide, alleviating the pain of depression, and other mental illnesses, to easing the pain of the sick, the lonely, isolated and aged, and to be available to desperate persons. They offer one of the best therapies known to mankind: the opportunity to talk freely about feelings and problems in strict confidence to someone who can listen with compassion and understanding. In the past ten years they have maintained a telephone befriending service seven days a week 24 hours a day; responded to roughly 250,000 calls from residents of Cape Cod and surrounding areas; recruited and trained over 315 volunteers and campaigned for the erection of steel barriers on the Sagamore and Bourne bridges over Cape Cod Canal which has virtually eliminated suicides from these bridges, provided speakers for 630 audiences, [and] provided emotional support to survivors of people who have committed suicide.

The Samaritans receive no funds from the federal government; the work is performed entirely by volunteers who generally average 30 hours of duty a month; operating expenses are financed mainly by private donations, plus a modest allocation from United Way. With the growing incidents of suicide among both the old and the young, with the failure of our mental health institutions to provide adequate health to all in need, with the increasing number of people living alone without family or friends to share in their problems, I urge my colleagues to join me in saluting the Samaritans of Cape Cod as we observe their tenth anniversary . . . and wish them many more years of providing a service of my district which is both unique and desperately needed.

The Boston branch of the Samaritans had been founded in 1974 by Monica Dickens and the Cape Cod branch was started in 1977. Throughout these years Dickens savored her role as Samaritan, novelist and homemaker.

Sadly, though, her husband, Roy, who had written two detective novels, including *The Decorated Corpse*, published by Mill and Morrow, 1962, died in 1985. That same year Dickens's *Miracles of Courage* (about the families of young children with deadly diseases) had been published, and Dickens began to think about returning to England permanently. Her most immediate novel after Roy's death, *Dear Doctor Lily* (1988), was described by some as an attempt to absolve herself for possibly neglecting Roy in favor of writing and pursuing the Samaritan dream. She sold the house in North Falmouth, Massachusetts, and it became a bed-and-breakfast, as it is to this day. Monica and Roy's daughter Prudence moved to Springfield, Massachusetts, where she became a legal secretary for a large insurance firm. Pamela traveled back to England, where she lives with her husband and 15-year-old twins in the cottage Monica moved to in 1986.

Rather quickly, she heard from her old colleagues that the leadership of the Cape Cod Samaritans had fallen on bad times. Ego trips, grandstanding, and personality conflicts marked what had once been a happy organization. She did not respond to these complaints, believing that they would naturally work themselves out. And so they did.

In England, Monica took up residence in a thatched cottage on Pudding Lane, in the village of Brightwalton, on the Berkshire Downs. There, she continued to live in her two worlds of novel-writing and the Samaritans.

At one of the annual meetings of the Samaritans, held in Yorkshire, she was the keynote speaker. She told her audience that, while the eighth principle of the Samaritans was a sense of humor, the ninth was that in practice sessions one became a better caller than volunteer. You play "the person in trouble" and make the people who "answer the telephone" believe it. In this speech, Monica talked, not about the *right* things to do when called, but about the *things not to do*. First, one must not probe for needless information. Stay on the subject. If a caller has no money and cannot pay his bills, *don't* say, "We can't handle that sort of thing;" instead, respond, "Let's see where you might get some help with this matter."

Of tremendous importance was for the volunteer to say something back to the caller other than "uh-uh" in response to a recitation of problems. One must not be a "grunter" in Samaritan circles. By being so, one becomes passive and puts too great a burden on the caller to do all the work. "People complain all the time that they never get anything back from their therapists, and that's why, so often, they call us." Samaritans can at least say, "that's amazing," "how terrible for you," or "so then what happened?"

Another function Monica Dickens saw to as a part of the Samaritans, was to participate in Chad Varah's "retirement" in late 1986—although, as she said, people like Chad Varah never retire. She wrote a poem entitled "Dear, There's No Escape."
She said:

> Dear Chad, you think you're casting off the chains
> You'll clean your desk and empty the wastebasket
> And flush the pictures of volunteer birds down the drains
> And not be there to answer when they ask it
> No more rush our trains from Barnes to Walbrook
> Suicide? What's that? Ask David or Simon
> I'm free to write in peace in my best of all book
> I've earned the comfortable retreat that I'm on
> Sorry, dear Chad, it doesn't work that way
> Samaritans are stuck in it like mud
> We who got into this mess are forced to say
>   it's in our hearts forever and our blood
> And so it is in yours that for each time a new befriending works
> It's because of what you've done

> Us vols and the desperate ones we help through you salute and love you.
> Darling No. 1; Monica 12.

Of course, Chad Varah did not "retire." He is still at it today (the mid 90s), still exercising his customary vigor in everything to which he sets his hand.

When she returned to England, Monica Dickens was not quite as active in Samaritan work as she had been previously, although she became a volunteer locally. She did, however, continue to write. Her works of the late 1980s included *Enchantment* and *Closed at Dusk* and *Scarred*. *Enchantment* was inspired by a tragedy in Hungerford, a village only six miles from her home, where several people were gunned down by the fantasy-driven Michael Ryan. The last novel she wrote was *One of the Family*, published just after her death, by Viking.

In late 1990 Monica Dickens fell ill with cancer of the colon. After her first operation she told a friend that she had now been reduced from an exclamation point to a semicolon. Despite continuous radiotherapy treatments at a hospital in nearby Reading, she continued to write. For two years she battled this cancer, but finally—on a Christmas day—she succumbed to it. She died in Dunedin Hospital on December 25, 1992. Obituaries appeared worldwide, some reflecting on the strange coincidence that the great granddaughter of Charles Dickens, author of *A Christmas Carol* died on this very holiday.

One might say that Monica Dickens had the best of four different worlds: comfort, curiosity, creativity, and caring.

Comfort, because she was born into comfortable circumstances. If she had been so inclined, she could have spent her entire life in high society.

But she had too much curiosity to be content with the circumstances of her birth, and perhaps she inherited this trait from her famous great-grandfather. What was the rest of the world like? What was just around the corner? Her life of curiosity superseded her life of comfort, and made her seek other social settings. Not that she rejected or even discounted the class into which she was born, but that, simply, interests—like those of her famous ancestor—were universal.

A creative person, a novelist, sees a difficult life situation, and in reporting it sometimes enlarges it in a way that will, perhaps, garner support for its alleviation. This is probably creativity at its best, because it becomes related to social reform. Monica always said she was a reporter; but she certainly was a reporter who had reforming uppermost in her mind.

And, finally, she was a *caring* person. When she told you something, you knew she meant it. There was no superficiality about her; she was the genuine article. As Sarah Hollis pointed out, Monica could make people about her feel important. And that, of course, is no small accomplishment today.

Monica Dickens was a quite extraordinary human being. She exemplified the thought that God gave us a brain, and He expects us to use it. Thus, she could not simply rely on whatever was tried, trusted, and true. Without ignoring or denying what others may have told her, her guiding force was to see things for herself.

Certainly she had all the fame and money she would ever need: fame from her ancestry and as a best-selling author in her own right, and money from her numerous publications. She definitely did not have to go into the Samaritans to compensate for any lack of self-confidence. She knew her strengths and weaknesses, and paid attention to both. Perhaps she went into the Samaritans because of the time-honored English tradition of those who are "high-born" giving something back to society for their privileged births.

It was a happy combination of inheritance and environment that produced such notable literary works in Monica Dickens, and at the same time such noble activities as she performed with the Samaritans.

CARLTON JACKSON

Befriending:

The American Samaritans

by

Monica Dickens

The man who, in a fit of melancholy, kills himself today,
would have wished to live had he waited a week.

—Voltaire

1

Since 1968, I have been working with the Samaritans. This is a vast
fellowship of ordinary men and women who offer to thousands of
suicidal, suffering and lonely people all over the world, the simple gift of
someone to talk to in confidence.

I originally volunteered with the Samaritans in London to get
material for a book I wanted to write. They knew this. They were willing
to have the book written, and to let me take what I needed from them
and pass on.

Usually, when you have lived with something for long enough to
write a book about it, you have consumed all its possibilities for you.
You have written it out of your system, and are glad to move on to
something else. After I had finished *The Listeners* [*End of the Line* in
America], my interest was increased rather than exhausted. I had become
absorbed in the work for its own sake.

I kept finding excuses to go back to London from America, where I
lived, so that I could return to the Samaritan center in the crypt of the
City Church of St. Stephens, Walbrook, where in rooms no bigger than a
medium-sized tomb, volunteers answered telephones and unhappy
visitors sought sanctuary among the ancient stones. I too needed the
company of those quiet-toned, undemanding Samaritans, and the
peculiarly satisfying experience of having nothing else to do but give
your full attention to somebody on the phone or sitting with you, who
really at that moment needs you. Not because of *who* you are, but
because of *what* you are: the person who is there for them.

We had a flat in London at that time, and each time I arrived there
from America, my first appointment was always with the Samaritans.
Once having reassured myself that I still belonged to that equable group
in the crypt, I could go about the other business for which I had come to
London, but whenever they could use me, I went to the Samaritan
center.

2 Befriending

I still remember vividly some of the people I talked to in those raw early days when I did everything wrong, and envied the experienced volunteers who seemed to do it right, and was surprised to find out that they were still nervous every time they picked up the emergency telephone, whose cry sounded so shrill and urgent between the crowding stones of the underground walls.

I remember a young man in a panic who should have been on his way to a new waiter's job, his sixth in five months. How was he going to cope with it? How was he going to keep it if his head fogged over and his hands shook like this? A runaway child with bright red hair, who came in with a dirty stuffed animal and sat speechless, her teeth clamped over her lower lip. The terrified woman whose divorced husband had told her calmly, with logical reasons, why he was going to kill himself today, and then hung up the phone with no indication of where he was. A young man from the North, alone and friendless in a west London hospital after a street fight.

I offered to visit him. A friend with a car drove me round looking for the hospital. The young man had got its name wrong. We tried all the hospitals in that area, and after two hours, the friend said, "Let's leave it."

"I promised to go."

"It's not your fault. He'll ring again and talk to someone else. Let's go and get something to eat."

At this point, being a new and very insecure Samaritan, the unknown boy in the hospital was much more important to me than the friend. There is a balance that has to be kept. When you promise to try to do everything you can to help, the words "try" and "can" are important. If you go disjointedly overboard for callers and put them before the people in your own life, you may end up being dependent on them, and that's no good for them or you.

Years later, an exhausted American woman, who was carrying most of the load one summer for a new Samaritan branch that was short of volunteers, told me that when she did escape for a swim, she imagined that the people on the beach were the people she talked to on the phone. She wanted them to be, because these were now the only people in her life.

That can also lead to savior fantasies, equally damaging, known among the volunteers as Instant Jesus, in which you believe not only that you are the only volunteer who can help, but that your victim cannot possibly survive without you. Or worse, that when they survive a suicidal crisis and courageously decide to have another try at life, the credit is yours for saving them.

If Samaritans befriended independently and were rung up or visited at home at any hour of the day or night, the service would collapse, and so would the Samaritans' lives. A large part of the effectiveness is that there are many and varied volunteers, some of whom are always instantly available. It is possible to go on being a Samaritan for years—for the rest of your life, if you can avoid fossilism and senility—if you share responsibility and avoid obsession. If volunteers resign because they are exhausted and burned dry, they have been doing it wrong, and you are better off without them.

After my friend had abandoned me in disgust, I did eventually find the young man, bandaged about the head in a small side-street clinic. He was not anxious, but surprised that I had come, because he had forgotten that I said I would. He did not want me to stay long, because he was watching television.

I remember the man who had run over his own child, and believed that his wife would suffer less if he were dead too. The destitute musician who had been sitting in St. Paul's, mustering his courage to go into the river, when he remembered that the Samaritans were somewhere near, and thought he would see if they had hot coffee. The soldier who deserted when he heard that his wife had taken the children and gone, found by a policeman at a railway station, and brought to us for help before the Military Police caught him. A disorganized young man who wanted to put his head in the gas oven, and begged us to come to him.

With Joe, another volunteer, I went into his flimsy little house cautiously, alert for gas. We found Danny's mother in bed with a bad back, a mountainous, cheerful woman who had seen her son through years of suicide attempts and arrests for petty crime, and many institutions. Joe and I sat on the other bed and Danny hopped into bed with his mother. He was sour and defeated. He told us about the men who followed him in the street and waited for him in doorways.

"They're going to kill me, so I'll kill myself first."

Joe, who was slow-spoken, started to go. "You sure you turned off that gas, Dan?"

As we talked on the beds, he traveled through aggression, fear, rage, hysterical tears to a sweet and tractable boyishness, laughing with us at harmless jokes. The vast mother mounded on the bed took every change of mood philosophically. Joe and I were superfluous.

There should have been an earth mother like this for Irene, or any mother except the preoccupied woman who vanished one day as if she had never existed. Admitted to the hospital after a serious suicide attempt, Irene had walked out with a stethoscope, not because she wanted it, but because she had to steal something to show she was still in control.

I went back with her to get her clothes and return the stethoscope, a long train journey into the outer suburbs, during which I heard about her disregarded life and the bitter self-disgust which made her try again and again to make an end to it, but never quite completely.

She would make a last-minute telephone call just before she passed out, take the pills on the back seat of a long-distance bus that stopped every three hours, cut her wrists in the ladies' room of a crowded cinema—and then castigate herself for failing.

"You see," she kept saying, "I can't do anything right. I make a mess of everything. I can't even kill myself."

"I'm glad."

"You're like everyone else. You want to condemn me to living."

I did not know what to say. I held her hand in the railway carriage, while she clutched the stethoscope in the other hand and cried, and the other passengers looked away.

I had never been riskily involved like this with people, been admitted into their lives at this kind of crisis. Even as a nurse, there was the buffer of the uniform, the hospital, the practical job to be done. I had never talked at such a depth, where defenses and pretenses are irrelevant, and anything can be said by either side.

I remember a bulky, breathless woman, an old friend of the Samaritans, some coat buttons missing, others in the wrong holes, who dropped in to pass the time of day and, since I was a new ear, told me something of past plights and dramas.

"You know Regina well?" I asked her, about the volunteer who had introduced us.

"Oh yes," she said casually. "I owe my life to Regina." And although Regina made suitable demurring sounds, I regarded her with awe and envy. Would anyone ever be able to think that about me?

It was these things that drew me so strongly to journey from Cape Cod to the tiny London flat in Kensington, and tugged me down through the dog mess and broken coke bottles to Gloucester Road station, where the announcement blackboard sometimes said, "Delay is due to body on line at . . ." to Cannon Street and up Walbrook to the Church.

In ordinary life, I had always felt awkward about offering help, intrusive, perhaps superfluous, certainly inadequate. Here in the crypt, I belonged to the structure of help.

The need to belong is very powerful. The loss of belonging can be a killer. The important element in the Samaritan response to suicidal people is the assurance of at least one person, for a start, to whom their life matters and to whom they belong, even for a short time, even for two hours in the middle of the night, when the pills are on the table and the bottle is half empty.

2

Perhaps it was because I needed a Samaritan branch to belong to that I decided to start the Samaritans in the United States. Perhaps it was because I had never forgotten the bulky woman with the missing coat buttons who owed her life to Regina.

An American volunteer in the London branch had said to me idly, between phone rings, "We ought to try to start this in the States." Although she was not serious, the remark stuck on me like a burr, and its seed germinated, in the way of chance ideas that are going to change your life.

Chad Varah, who founded the Samaritans in London in 1953, was encouraging. He had seen his original idea grow and spread to branches all over the United Kingdom and in many other countries. He would like to see the Samaritans in every country in the world.

Others were more dubious.

"In *America?* You could never make it work. Everyone has their own shrink there, you know. They'd ignore a service that wasn't professional. And the professionals would fight you, because they'd think you were trying to steal their customers."

"Would you ever get any volunteers? As I understand it, Americans won't do anything they don't get paid for. What *about* money anyway? I hear they're taxed to death, and the rich give only to whatever's fashionable, like sickle cell anemia and whales."

In Britain, if you wanted to start a new branch of the Samaritans, you would have to have help from headquarters, and although you would have the local tasks of finding money and volunteers and a center, people would know what you were talking about, and would have at least a rough idea of what you were planning to do.

When I started tentatively to explore my chances in Boston, I had first to explain what the Samaritans did as a whole, and then what I was trying to do as a microcosm.

"Befriending, eh? Sounds like a great idea. What does it mean? I see. Active listening. Like psychiatrists do. How will you get enough qualified people to work with you? Ordinary people? Oh . . . volunteers. I've had some experience with them at the hospital. They're unreliable. Most of them are either social climbers, or senile. Yours would be supervised, of course, by professionals? You can't let volunteers loose on patients, except to collect money for the television or wheel them down to X ray."

"What can you do on the phone? I can see that talking helps, but you can get just so—they come *in*? And volunteers go to see *them*? Taking a bit of a risk, wouldn't it be? This is a violent society we live in, Miz Digguns."

"Of course you'll use the opportunity of their crisis to bring them back to God. Not a religious organization . . . I see."

"Of course you'll have to set up the phones so that you can trace calls and interviews. How is your relationship with the police?"

The few negatives are more memorable than the positives, because they hurt and daunt you, when you are experimenting. There were, of course, marvelously receptive people who did not say any of those things, who listened encouragingly to what I see now may have looked like the unpractical obsession of a crazy Englishwoman with a glittering eye.

Being English, crazy or sane, does help, however. Many people in New England feel a sneaking impulse, often against their will, to admire the British, and to suspect that we may possess some valuable secret.

Right or wrong, I find this very touching. I have heard people in England being gratuitously insolent to Americans, as if it didn't matter, like kicking the cat. I remember when my husband, Roy, was in England and we were engaged, how some people moved in to attack him about American foreign policy and other things that were not his fault, before they even said that they were glad we were going to be married, which some of them were not.

No one has ever been rude to me in America just for being English, except drunken Samaritan callers who will fasten onto anything to feed a wretched grievance, and will ring back off and on all night to call me and the Queen a pair of bloody limeys, before they pass out.

Although I was glad of this subconscious respect for my obsessive idea just because it was English, I had to be careful to emphasize that I was trying to develop from within Boston something that was needed and natural, not trying to impose something foreign from outside.

This was explained to me by the first of the many people who actively helped me—Dr. Rollin Fairbanks, a professor at the Episcopal Divinity School in Cambridge, who taught and wrote about all aspects of death, including suicide. [Dr. Fairbanks died in 1989—ed.]

Cambridge, just across the Charles River from Boston, is a town of eighteenth century [style] expansive wooden houses on wide leafy streets, with smaller houses jostling in the side streets round Harvard

Square, cut up into as many apartments and little shops as possible, since everybody wants to live there, or to sell enticing things to those who do. The reputable red brick of Harvard is there, and the white Wren church spires, and the austere magnificence of the Massachusetts Institute of Technology, and the reassuring English Gothic of the Episcopal Divinity School, just down the road from Longfellow's mansion.

I met Rolly Fairbanks in the cafeteria, a big bear of a man with a limp, and we ate tuna fish, potato salad, cottage cheese, and sweet pickles. The director of an English Samaritan branch had studied here with him the year before, so his listening was informed, as well as civil, and his interest was strong.

"I know there's a need," he said. "Professionals often feel too anxious and helpless to respond quietly and compassionately to suicidal people. They either back off, or want to take over. And social service agencies aren't set up to deal with despair. The loneliness, the need to reach out, the cry—" he looked at me gravely. "Is there anybody out there who cares?"

"That's *it*." I was excited. "That's what we want to be."

"I know," Rolly said. "I want to help."

At that early stage, when I was a lone wolf who had bitten off half an elephant, anyone who would listen and approve was encouraging. Someone who would throw in his lot with me was a hero. I drove the seventy miles back to Cape Cod with my mind racing ahead into my favorite fantasy of a subterranean Samaritan center, where men and women sat at a long shelf, murmuring gently into telephones, and other phones were ringing. I saw the life-lines thrown out by us to the unknown them, who grabbed and were pulled in closer.

With Rolly saying, "I want to help," the Center was already in operation, as far as I was concerned.

He suggested that our best start might be to gather a group together at the divinity college, explain the concept of the Samaritans, and let them interpret it domestically.

With people he knew and people I was discovering, we would have a group of about fifty, including an English Samaritan named Michael teaching at a New York university, who agreed to come and back me up.

A good start, except that some time before, I had asked a plastic surgeon to whittle away my baggy Dickensian eyelids, and he now announced that the only time he could possibly fit it in was a few days before the date on which we had invited all these people to the meeting. Fifty people had been invited and sixty came, which was exhilarating, even though I did appear to have been hit by a bus or punched in a brawl. Vainly, I wore large, dark glasses to cover up my black eyes.

It was the first time I had spoken in public without being able to see the audience, to watch the reactions, note who is nodding approval and who is frowning, who is quick to pick up a joke, who is nodding because they're asleep, and where the potential allies and troublemakers are.

I had to throw the Samaritans out into the dark void, with no idea what people were thinking. Michael added his very English, unassuming: "Not used to speaking . . . who am I, an ordinary volunteer. . . don't know if I helped anyone. The others did though. Proud to be one of them." Gentlemanly and pleasant, no harm done.

I don't quite know what results I expected from this meeting. I always hoped, in those early days before we got organized, that each meeting, each new contact would somehow magically put the pieces into place and make things start to happen. Gradually, through disappointing myself by expecting too much, I began to learn that no single event or person would be the magic key, and that the talks and contacts, the endless telephone calls to people who were always "in conference"— i.e., chatting to someone—were part of the whole slow, cumulative move forward.

At the end of the meetings, audiences asked questions, gave opinions, discussed ideas—often more academic than practical—on how this amiable British notion of befriending suicidal people might be adapted to the swifter, skilled world of Boston.

We could be an outreach arm of the emergency mental health system. We could attach ourselves to one of the large downtown churches. We should affiliate with a university counseling clinic. We must be supervised by one of the state human service agencies. Michael looked worried. My eyes began to twitch and flicker, and I wanted to tear off the dark glasses and rub at the scars to counterattack them with lusty pain.

The meeting was getting away from me. I did not want to attach myself to anybody. I did not want government money. I did not know how to start a simple Samaritan branch, let alone an outreach arm of the emergency mental health system.

Out of the audience, like a well-scrubbed hero in a fairy tale, stepped an unlikely hero—one of Rolly's protégés, a young psychiatrist with clean hair and a fresh child's face, who asked, "Why can't we stay with grass roots? This seems to work well in England. Why can't it be tried in the same way here?"

It seemed simpler to agree with him than to spend any more time trying to fit the Samaritans into the social service or religious networks.

The audience began to leave, satisfied that they had given the nod to doing something about suicide, whether or not I was ever heard from again.

My eyes were on fire. I went home and wept. I thought that the lids would never heal, but I persevered with iced cloths, so that when ultimately the surgeon did take out the stitches, he praised me for having less bruising and scarring than any of his other eyelid revisions.

The day after getting rid of the stitches, I telephoned Stuart, the clean psychiatrist, to ask if he would join a steering committee with half a dozen people from the meeting: friends of mine or Rolly's, a graduate student who had done a paper on suicide, a minister who had worked with the Samaritans in Singapore. We met at a friend's house in Cambridge, and I hoped they would know what committees did, because I did not.

My original naive idea had been to gather a few volunteers, prepare them with the help of some training material from England, get enough money to put in a phone, and start as soon as possible.

If I had done that, we might have lasted a few months, just long enough to collect a few desperately needy callers who trusted us, before we disappeared from the scene, leaving the desperate ones to hear, "I'm sorry. The number you have called is not in service."

Now, ten years later, when the Samaritans U.S.A has been organized nationally to help new branches and see that they don't open before they are ready, I see my old self mirrored in the eager pioneers from different towns who argue, "But we want to get started helping people, not have more meetings and write funding proposals. What if someone dies whom we might have helped to live?"

That was the way I felt. That was the way Chad had done it, with a few people who had originally dropped into St. Stephen's, Walbrook, to make tea and sit with the distressed people waiting to see him. If he had waited until he had fifty trained volunteers, and two years funding, the Samaritans would never have started. If I had waited in Boston until I had everything just so and knew what I was doing, perhaps we would never have got started either, although I do see now that once an organization is established and growing, you can't keep lurching along in a hit-or-miss shoestring way.

The committee decided that we should hold a larger public meeting and invite a lot of the right kind of people, to try to get volunteers, money, publicity, and approval from Boston professionals who wanted to see something done about the rising rate of suicide. There had once been a one-man suicide prevention service called Rescue, run with spectacular bravery and devotion by Father Kenneth Murphy, who would charge out with a flashing red light on his car to bridges and high buildings, and talk people down. Now that he had gone back to a parish, exhausted, there was a void for the suicidal, which we hoped in our modest way to fill.

A public meeting can work well in a small town, where people may go to meetings for want of anything else to do, and have the time to be curious, at least, about new projects. In a big, busy city, it's chancy. I did not know that at the time, and felt buoyed up by the belief that if we invited about a thousand people, four or five hundred would come.

It was April, 1973. I thought we could have the meeting in June. Oh no, said the Bostonians in the group, no one does *anything* in the summer. No one is here in the summer anyway. We'll wait until September or October.

Five or six months! I was dashed. But since these Boston people were the ones who seemed to know everybody, and I knew nobody, I had to agree.

I spent my summer typing lists and envelopes, collecting names from the committee and anyone else who would help, looking up addresses and chafing. To keep my enthusiasm nourished, I read all the esoteric material sent me from the Samaritans in England, and was glad I had not read it last December when my idea became action, because it showed me how much I did not know. How much careful selection, training, supervision and knowledge must lie behind what looks like the simple business of having a constant supply of the right kind of volunteers at the end of the telephone!

By the beginning of October, few people had answered the invitation, and most of those could not come.

"People don't commit themselves," the committee told me. "You have no way of knowing."

Would the auditorium we had borrowed at Children's Hospital be big enough for a crowd? Or too big for a handful?

I was not simply nervous on that night. I was anguished. We had burned our boats. Mistake or not—spending all that time getting together the impressive list of people whose secretaries had probably fluttered the invitations unread into the wastepaper basket—we had to go through with it.

I was too jittery to greet or talk to the people who did come. I remember a doctor who had traveled all the way from an outlying cancer hospital to tell me his ideas about suicide in terminally ill patients. I could not make myself stand still to listen to him. For some crazed reason, it became more important for me to open a box of meaningless leaflets and distribute them on seats that were not going to be filled.

I had talked in many places in different countries. I had made speeches about Charles Dickens and about myself all over the United States for the easy lecture circuit buck. Why did I fall apart now when I needed all that brash confidence that sustained me in Grand Forks, North Dakota, and Indianapolis, Indiana?

At this point, the Samaritans hardly seemed relevant. This folly was not related to sitting with a telephone pressed to your ear and sharing someone's misery. A trickle of people had come in and spaced themselves through the auditorium as if they were infectious. Eight p.m. Eight ten. We waited. There must be more. There were not.

Now that it had happened, the agony of uncertainty was over. I could slump in the empty front row, gray with the knowledge of doom. Avery Wiseman, Harvard professor and senior psychiatrist at Massachusetts General Hospital, spoke intelligently about suicide and the need for help, but my pride in having him there was spoiled by the fear that he must be thinking, "They cajoled me here—for *this*?"

The English Samaritan who had come over to give the main talk must have been thinking the same thing. He was courteous, in a diffident British way, and understated, as Samaritans are supposed to be. The audience listened with equal courtesy, because he was English, but I could feel them already half on their way to getting out of there and never giving the Samaritans another thought.

By the time I had to stumble through an appeal for volunteers and money, I had already realized not only that you don't raise money this way but that no one in the small audience was likely to think of volunteering.

They were, however, thinking of other things. When questions began, some people—not the few blacks in the audience—asked quite aggressively what we planned to do about ensuring a racial balance of volunteers.

"Well . . . we'll see who applies. I'm not sure that it matters if—"

"It matters. You can't start until you have recruited as many black volunteers as white."

Thin murmurs of assent. Was I insane not to have thought of this? Did it only show how unfit I was to try to start this service in a land still alien to me after more than twenty years?

If I had obeyed the aggressive injunction and waited for total integration, we would not have the Samaritans yet in America. We have excellent black volunteers and many black people who call for help; but not as many of either as we would like, and perhaps there never will be.

There were the expectable complaints that suicidal people are mentally ill and need only professional therapy, that suicide prevention has no effect on statistics, some other doubts, and a small amount of scattered approval. Then a young man with a ginger [colored], or red, beard and jerkin stood up in the back row. He said that he represented a Boston hot line, which I knew as a youth center for drug problems, and announced, swaying groggily with bummed-out eyes, that any suicide problems in the city could be handled by his hot line, and they could do it without middle-class amateurs muscling in.

I went cold. When you are nervous and disappointed anyway, that sort of thing is all you need to make you want to call the whole thing off.

A young woman with a sad and beautiful face tersely answered the ginger man:

"Are you afraid they'll compete for your funding, or are you scared they'll steal your clients? There's room in this city for as much help as possible."

Hooray.

Two people applauded her. Others turned to stare or mutter at the ginger jerkin, and I learned an important lesson.

When you are speaking about something emotional, like suicide, and you are attacked from the audience, don't risk making a fool of yourself, or the attacker. Let the audience answer. If someone says something outrageous or insulting or idiotic, it's better to ask the audience impartially, "What do the rest of you think about that?" and let them tell each other, "That's absurd."

The young man and his friends milled about in the lobby for a while, complaining and arguing. Later on, we all became friends, and they began to refer suicidal people to us, and we referred drug problems and runaways to them. The beautiful girl with the sad pure face became one of our first volunteers.

The meeting was not a complete fiasco. A journalist, Jean Dietz, was there from the *Boston Globe*. She had left early, and I feared that she had written us off, but she wrote for us a clever and perceptive feature: "Hope Springs for the Critically Despondent." That was just what we needed. She even used the small audience to illustrate the point that no one cared.

The article produced inquiries from would-be volunteers. It brought me Rosemary, a social worker between jobs who let us use a room in her house for an office, and helped me with the mysteries of incorporation and tax exemption.

It brought me Sally, a young volunteer who had survived a suicidal crisis herself and wanted to help someone else to survive. When

Rosemary and I interviewed her, she told us everything about her despair, and the knife-edge of danger on which she had balanced, afraid to die, and terrified of living.

Years later, I asked her why she had revealed so much. "Did you trust us?"

"I thought you didn't seem to know much about suicide, so I'd better tell you."

The newspaper article also brought us our first caller. Lily sat by the window of Rosemary's house on Beacon Hill, looking out at the well-dressed mothers fetching their children from the little school opposite on Brimmer Street. She spoke of guilt, and old memories she needed to talk about that were too terrible to discuss.

Lily had been in therapy, and in and out of hospitals for years. When she read the story in the *Globe*, she thought it was a new answer. She thought that perhaps in some way we could deflect the driving force that constantly urged her to kill herself, and try it again and again.

She sat in a straight chair in a bright red coat with a prim collar, and a stunning orange hat, and showed me pictures of herself as a girl, which she pretended were taken last year. She did seem pleased to be able to talk, although I was confounded as to what was wrong, or what I could do to help.

In those days, I thought I had to *do* something, to find instant solutions and acceptable answers—the delusion with which many new Samaritans try to clothe the naked anxiety of their inadequacy. So when Lily centered her narrative on the present, and fretted about the creaking shop sign below her window and the knocking in the radiator with which, she was sure, the landlord sought to torment her, I grabbed at her story.

"Why don't you complain?"

"I dare not."

Did she want me to speak to the landlord, or the owner of the sign?

Oh *no*! What did I want to do—get her into trouble?

I had to learn, and I am learning still that when people complain about something that is nothing to do with you—or even if it is—they don't want you to spring into action on their behalf. They want you to listen, and to siphon off some of the grievance by hearing it.

I dredged up another solution. Air in the pipes. I had seen the plumber bleed the old radiators at home of hissing hot water. I borrowed a wrench, and we walked slowly up the red brick heights of Beacon Hill to Lily's one room apartment. Outside the window, a rusted sign creaked gently. The screw at the bottom of the radiator was impossible to turn.

Kneeling, I looked up at Lily, standing by the chest of drawers in her girlish coat and flamboyant hat.

"I'll bring some oil next time, and some more tools."

"No."

She pulled open the long middle drawer. Getting up, I saw that it was crammed with boxes and little bottles: thousands of pills, to kill herself.

There were piles of clean folded linen and towels on the two chairs and on the table, so I moved to sit on the bed, which was stripped to the frame and mattress. Lily screamed, and, when I jumped up, explained that if I touched anything in the room, she would have to spend hours cleaning it. She had not wanted me to touch the radiator, but did not know how to say so. Now she would have to scrub it.

She told me what it was like to live as an obsessive-compulsive. If she bought a new blouse, she had to wash it eight times before she could wear it. Each day at four p.m., she must be back in her room to start the washing rituals, which took four hours to complete. Standing up, both of us, in the middle of the room, she showed me her fine bony hands. They were raw.

Lily and I met several times after that, and got to know each other quite well. We went out to lunch, and she showed me stories she had written, and told me jokes. When we opened our center, she rang up almost every day and got to know different volunteers, or came in for coffee, bringing her own mug and a cushion to sit on.

She became very fond of Sally, who saw her often and learned some of her tragic history and her horrifying experiences in a state mental hospital, and what it was like to live with suicide as a daily choice.

Sally allowed Lily to worry about her—whether she had a warm jacket, enough food, enough sleep—a favor you can sometimes do for someone who is tired of always worrying about themselves, for want of anyone else to worry about. When someone has been imprisoned in their own sadness and anxiety and the self-absorption of self-dislike, and they discover the energy to say, "You look tired. What time have you been going to bed?" you are entitled to feel more hopeful about them.

3

Chad Varah came over to visit during the long summer months of frustrated waiting, when there was "nobody in Boston," and trailed around with me to some of the people who might help, who passed us to someone else, who passed us on again.

I learned—much of the story of early days is about learning, but when you know nothing, learning is all there is to do—that the people who are really going to give you time and energy come to you, not by being pursued, but of their own accord, to move you forward.

Mostly I plodded along, doing what I thought had to be done each day. There were times, though, when the task seemed too enormous, my ignorance too vast, the gap too wide between my easy dream of volunteers murmuring into phones, and the complex reality of what had to be known and done to start any kind of organization, let alone one that dealt with life and death.

Every time I thought I could not do it, and dared even to consider the contemptible relief of giving it up and not having to try any more, someone would turn up out of the blue, like Stuart, like Rosemary, like Sally who could type and set up files, and say, "This is what you do now," and I would have to go on.

My life was already in shreds, my friends abandoned, my horse unridden, my garden unweeded, my house uncleaned, my writing put aside, my husband neglected. I drove the seventy miles to and from Boston almost every day.

When I told Chad in the early days, "I can't do it," he would answer, "All you need is moral courage."

I tell that now to people who are trying to start new branches. It is no practical help, but it makes you feel better about what you lack.

Chad also said, "Get your volunteers together and put them to work."

So Rosemary and Sally and I began to interview people who were interested. After declining the aggressives, and the saviors of the world, and the amateur psychologists with jargon to match, and the non-stop talkers, and the people who had really come to unload their own dramas and difficulties, we ended up with fifteen volunteers. Robin worked in a

17

drug program. Pat was a television producer. Dennis was blind. Karen was an airline stewardess, Fran an artist. Jim was a medical student. Jean could do book-keeping. And there were other pioneers willing to take a chance with us.

I went on the first television talk show where I promoted the Samaritans instead of my own books. The other guest with me was a sex therapist. She got most of the camera time, since she demonstrated her techniques by grabbing the hand of the wary young man who was interviewing us and placing it, resistant, on the inside of her trousered thigh, or on her pendant bosom. Suicide and befriending had nothing to do with that.

Barbara from the agency sponsoring the sex therapist had asked me a lot of questions at the studio, and had a face I could not forget. I rang her the next day and asked her if she would work with us, and heard that she too had been through her own suicidal crisis.

Before the Samaritans, I had no idea how many people have brushes with suicide. Now I realize that about half of us have probably given it serious thought, and that just about all of us may at least consider it at some time in our lives.

That doesn't mean that we're going to do it. But we could, if things got too bad. "It is always consoling," Nietzsche said, "to think of suicide: in that way one gets through many a bad night."

Barbara, Sally, Jean and I, and the others met every week in the house of a psychologist who had worked with the Samaritans in London. Stuart, the clean psychiatrist, came and talked about depression, Rosemary talked about the social service system, and I made up the rest of the training course from what I read and remembered of classes in London, although I had slept through a lot of them, having usually just got off a transatlantic plane.

Get your volunteers and put them to work. The incorporation and tax exempt papers came through, still Greek to me, even after I had filled them in. We made the committee into a Board of Directors, and added a lawyer, a teacher, a rabbi, and some other citizens of good will. Who should be President? No one wanted to be President.

"I know this man," said the graduate student who had written a paper on suicide. "He's a businessman. He'd know how to run a meeting."

He came to our first Board meeting. When it was announced to him that he was to be elected President of our hopeful little group, he stood up in my friend's house, knocking over a small table of ashtrays and knick-knacks and delivered an impassioned speech in favor of suicide, on the grounds that if people were crazy enough to want to do it, the world was better off without them. He nodded politely and walked out, leaving the graduate student to find her own way home.

Somebody was shaken enough to offer to be President. Someone else wouldn't mind being Treasurer for a year; Sally could be Secretary because she could type, and we were off. We had collected a little money. Now we had to find a place to put in a telephone and advertise the number.

As well as the people who moved me forward, there were also those who tried to hold me back. Some of the Board members were scared of moving out of the planning stage and doing anything as foolhardy as talking to an actual client. We should not be seeing anyone like Lily, or taking any calls that were not on business.

"I'm going to kill myself."

"Is this a business call?"

"I'm going to blow my brains out."

"I'm sorry, we're not open."

Bang!

Sometimes it was hard to tell whether a call to Rosemary's house was purely for business or for information, or whether the caller really needed to talk. We began to discover that if you shut up and listen, it gives people the chance to get to the reason why they called.

"I need some information about suicide for a thesis," may be genuinely a request for some statistics, facts, or ideas about adolescent suicide; but it may equally be a desperate young person trying to see if we will listen, who has chosen suicide as her subject because that is what is on her mind a lot of the time.

We began to learn to be less business-like with business callers, and to ask, "Is there anything else?" before ending a fairly routine conversation. I was surprised at how often there was something else. But why should I be surprised? Wasn't this the reason I wanted to start the Samaritans in Boston in the first place?

Other faint hearts still thought we should have our center in a psychiatric clinic, or only talk to people referred to us by doctors and social workers, or attach ourselves to one of the big hospitals—befriend people who were waiting in the Emergency Room, or were families of patients. Safer that way, and we could all wear pink smocks and have "Samaritan" on a laminated chest label to distinguish us from the hospital volunteers who worked in the gift shop, and mustn't be sorrowed at.

A high-powered lady, invited to a Board meeting as an expert on something or other, announced confidently that we should not open for another two years, if then. If we collected a few thousand dollars, she said, we must spend it on an in-depth area survey to analyze if there was a "Felt Need"—she said it in capitals—for such a service as ours.

We sat stunned, as you do when you don't know whether to laugh or cry, and the voice of authority is coming through its hat.

"I know there is a need."

"How?"

"You uncover it when you . . ." I said. "In England."

"The United States is not England," she was glad to be able to reassure us.

She left then, and we thought afterward that perhaps she had wanted to be the person who was paid to do the two year survey.

If you had to assess a need, felt or otherwise, the simplest way must be to put in a telephone and see if anybody called.

I wandered the streets of Boston in the central area around the Commons and the Public Gardens and the bus station, and looked at office space at astronomical rents, where volunteers would not be allowed in or out of the building after six p.m. I saw nasty angled rooms in converted houses with years of dirt and carpet stains and torn paper in them. In vain, I asked some of the social agencies for even just one room.

Walking past the old Arlington Street Unitarian Church on the busy kaleidoscopic corner of Arlington and Boylston Streets, I remembered that Rolly Fairbanks had told me that the minister here had studied death and dying with Elizabeth Kübler-Ross, and was interested in suicide.

I went up the brownstone steps into the church office, and asked if I could see him.

"He's with some people."

"Can I wait?"

She rang upstairs. "He'll see you."

She put me into a tiny lift, or elevator, and pressed a button. It was only when you stopped that you realized it had been moving. As I stepped out, an enormous black man in a clerical collar squeezed down the narrow passage with his arms out to welcome me.

His name had been Renford Gaines, but he was now Mwalimu Imara, the first black minister of any of the big old Back Bay churches, once fashionable, now two-thirds empty. He had lost some more of its congregation by haranguing them in his sermons for being white, although they had done their best by appointing him, but had added to its already racy reputation for enterprising liberalism.

He had a group of young people with him, discussing things like revolution, and they welcomed me too, and we all sat down and talked about the Samaritans.

"This would be a good place for us to start."

I was half joking, but Mwalimu was interested, and I have had enough luck in my life to recognize its approach.

"We've had street people, draft resisters, drugs, Women's lib—the people here will kill me if I bring another group in." But he did offer to let us use the small brightly polished chapel to train volunteers.

So that I would not be in the preacher's place, the volunteers turned their chairs around and sat with their backs to what would be the alter if Unitarian chapels had altars, and we talked of suicide, depression, alcohol, sex, and grief, while the organist at his evening practice made chimes and joyful thunder in the great church beyond the whispering leather [hung] door.

During the last class, Mwalimu came in and said that he had something for us. He led us downstairs, and there it was—the Samaritan Center I had seen in fantasy, not exactly as I had imagined, but instantly recognizable, a long low basement room, with its own entrance at the bottom of the outside steps.

"We could use it?"

"They'll kill me," Mwalimu said in his broad, smiling voice. "But you can have it free, until you get enough money to start paying rent."

The Arlington Street Church was built in 1861 for a congregation descended from a tiny group of immigrant Scottish Calvinists. A hundred years later, the brownstone church, modeled on St. Martin-in-the-Fields for the respectable Boston Unitarians, had become famous for taking chances on "disreputable" people.

In the late sixties, street people came in for help with drugs, and a crowd of very young runaways who hung about on the Commons with the hippies and winos slept in the church every night. A soldier absent without leave from the Vietnam draft was given sanctuary in the church until he was dragged out by military police. A service was held for draft resisters, during which they burned their draft cards at an altar candle before the congregation and the television cameras.

Although the Samaritans are neither religious, political, nor activist, we felt that we fit into Arlington Street Church history. And it fit ours. The shabby basement of an old church—what a suitable destination for my dream that had started its journey from the crypt of St. Stephen's, Walbrook.

Our room had a table and chairs, some torn posters from the sixties, and a bulletin board on legs which we could put across one corner, for privacy. We could not use the wide fireplace, but it was reassuringly domestic. We cleaned out the cigarette stubs and yellowed papers and dried cat turds which former occupants had left in the grate. We washed the window and swept the littered steps and scrubbed the dirt-clotted linoleum and laid down the old carpet from my kitchen. Somebody's mother gave us a green plastic armchair, which we put over the floor scars of burning popcorn oil.

Beyond a glass inner door, the secrets of the church basement dwelled in winding passages, locked doors and abandoned church schoolrooms with miniature chairs askew at the sawn-off tables and paint water still in mugs, as if the children had been kidnapped. To get to the lavatories far away at the back of the alley door, you went past a huge kitchen with a massive iron grill and potato mixer, like parts of an old locomotive, and through a dark hall with a stage, filled with booby traps to stumble over while you grasped for a light switch.

Upstairs, the orderly business of the church went on. Mwalimu's deep laugh, and gusts of organ music came down the stairs as from another world.

We did everything in our room—answered the telephone, held meetings, interviewed and trained more volunteers, and half killed with befriending any stranger who came innocently down the steps to sell us personalized book matches, or tell us a car was illegally parked.

When Chad had needed money to keep the Samaritans going in London in the early days, he used to pray for it, and someone would die and leave him a thousand pounds. We took a more secular route through insurance companies and business offices and banks. The small brave graduate student tried her hand at writing a funding proposal—a complicated procedure for which the experts said you had to go back to college to learn—and a foundation gave us ten thousand dollars.

No holding back now. We had twenty-two volunteers. On April 4th, 1974, five months since I had told that disastrous public meeting that we would not open until we had a hundred volunteers, five years since I heard the woman with the missing coat buttons say, "I owe my life to Regina," we announced that the Samaritans in Boston was open for business.

Interviewed by newspapers, television and radio stations, I tried to sound as if I knew what I was talking about. Now that I know a bit more about suicide in all its varieties, and that each one is different, I know much less, in a way, than I thought I did when I knew very little.

Fortunately, nobody really listens when you pontificate on the air, or remembers your quoted assertion in newspapers: "Social forces have no effect on suicide rates, Dickens asserts." The publicity coalesced into some kind of message about suicide, and announced a number that anyone could call at any time for any reason. Quite soon, the telephone began to ring, with proof enough of the need in Boston for someone to talk to.

4

Our first emergency cry for help came to the volunteer I had met with the television program hands-on sex therapist. When Barbara picked up the telephone, the weak voice of an old lady told her that she was alone and penniless, with nothing in the house but half a box of rice. She had tidied up her papers, left a letter for her daughter in Seattle, sent her cat to be put to sleep, and now her last job was to put a plastic bag over her head.

Her radio was on—"The only voice I hear"—and when she heard our number advertised, she thought that she would make just one call to see if anyone in the world cared whether an old lady put a plastic bag over her head. She was going to ring off, but Barbara was able to hold her long enough to secure the contact between them, and the tears and the words poured out—and the despair.

I wish every cry for help were as easy to answer. Carol, who lived nearby, took food to the old lady, and then went to her Social Security office and found that two thousand dollars were due to her in undelivered payments.

"Why didn't she call this office?" they asked.

Old people are afraid of bureaucracy, of the telephone, of making a mistake, of being a nuisance. Even now that the Samaritans are well known, it is still hard to reach old people with the idea that we are there for them, even when nothing is wrong, except the need to hear another voice. When they do ring, they often start with, "I hope I'm not bothering you. There must be others worse off than me."

We did not have enough volunteers, so at first we had an answering service to cover the nights. If callers would give their number, the operator would telephone whichever one of us was on call, and we would ring the person back.

Although I have talked to thousands of people since, I remember very clearly many of the callers of those long-ago nights when I jumped out of bed to answer the phone in the next room before it woke anybody, and sat and shivered on the floor by the tepid radiator, because I had not had time to bring the eiderdown with me.

Answering the telephone at night in the center is not very different from the daytime, except that it is more secret and peaceful. At home at night with the house asleep, there was a special urgent intensity, as if we were the only two people alive in a dead world. Some of the callers I talked to on those anxious nights were friends for a long time.

Tom, whom I kept seeing on and off for years, started off with, "I'm going to do it tonight," and hung up, but not before giving his telephone number. I had to ring him back three times before he would answer.

He lived on the fringes of bars and murky rackets, and hated his life and hated himself, his alcoholism and homosexuality, and had nobody in the world remotely concerned with whether he lived or died.

When people tell you that, it often turns out that there really is someone—perhaps several people—but because the spirit's gray overcast lets only negative messages in or out, it seems to the sufferer as if they don't care, and would be better off if he or she were dead.

As I got to know Tom, I understood that what he said was true. It was strange and unreal to be his only person in the world on those cold New England nights in April, when I clutched the telephone on the floor, unable to leave it to turn up the heat or get a blanket, because when he was drinking and suicidal, he might go away from the phone and leave it off the hook so that I could not call him back.

Late one night, a frightened woman rang to say that her neighbor had come beating on the door, with a towel around the wrist she had begun to cut. She had left her violent husband, and wanted only to die.

Nancy was sobbing and screaming, but desperate enough to grab onto some kind of lifeline between us. She rang almost every night, and different volunteers sustained her through different ordeals of crisis and despair, and after a while, she dropped the preliminaries of, "I can't talk about it . . . shouldn't have called . . . you're angry with me. . . ." and let one of us go to see her.

Tom and Nancy and some of the other people we talked to on the telephone began to come in to our one-room center under the church. On a sprung and sagging sofa from the Goodwill thrift shop, we sat with them behind the bulletin board, then behind an old backdrop curtain from a television studio, which we hung from the ceiling. That was better, but still not ideal. The sexton's favorite entrance to the windowless cell where he slept was in this corner. We could not persuade him to use the other door.

"Don't mind me." With brooms and buckets, he pushed in and out around the curtain, past weeping women and glum men and confused ranters.

This corner also had our room's only window. It looked out onto a noxious well at the bottom of the basement steps, where street dwellers who hang about on that variegated corner of Boston, and lie with wine bottles on the soiled summer grass of the Public Garden, had for years slept and urinated and left their broken bottles and disintegrated bits of clothing.

Hairy faces peered blearily in at the sofa through the rusted window grill. New volunteers coming down the steps in the early morning would report that there was a dead body in the well.

Some of these men began to come in, when they found out we had free coffee. At first when we were not busy, we welcomed them, and were starry-eyed enough to talk about A.A. and detoxification centers, which they endured, as a fair price for a mug of coffee.

It was difficult to get rid of people who moved in to stay with their shopping bags and spiky umbrellas, or became aggressive, or peed or vomited on the green plastic chair or the chintz sofa. You can ask people to leave, but if you lay a hand on them to pull them up or steer them to the door, it's legal assault. They know that.

Brian, who had been on that corner for years, came in wearing a long gray clerical overcoat, with tales of his well-born and successful past, and of his yearning to get sober and back to professional life. When Pat asked him where he got the money to drink so much, he laid his handsome head of filthy hair in his hands and wept at the shame of telling her that he was a male prostitute.

True or not, the pity of it got him a cup of the soup we had going in the church kitchen, and he settled in the broken armchair to entertain the volunteers with outrageous stories. After that, he came back nearly every day with stray dogs that threw up on our carpet, or gifts of broken clocks, or wallets thrown away after the contents had been rifled.

As we grew busier, Brian and the others were an embarrassment. If we would not let him in, he would go around to the alley behind the church and come back with a bundle of wire coat-hangers from the cleaners, or a dying plant thrown out by the flower shop. I still have a stunted palm tree in a tin tub with which he lurched into the center one day when we were trying to impress a monied visitor with how well organized we were. It has never grown, but it has never quite died either.

If people could not come to us, we tried to go to them, if it looked like an emergency. As I had only lived in the countryside, Boston was still a strange city to me, and I did not know which parts were safe, and which were not.

28 Befriending

The first person I went out to see was a man who said he was going to cut his throat, and this time he would do it right, and not end up in the hospital. I took another volunteer with me because I was scared, not of the strange neighborhood, or of the man with the razor blade, but of not knowing how to help him, or of getting there too late.

The razor blade was in his pocket. While we talked, he took it out and played with it, and drew the edge lightly over his wrist, to see it followed by little beads of blood. After two hours, he gave the razor blade to Paul, and lay down on his bed and began to sigh very deeply. Paul spent the night with him, and the next day, he began to pick up shreds of hope, and to be able to look at other things he might do with his predicament, besides cutting his throat.

Sally ventured into the Combat Zone, an ugly place of bars and strip joints to find a despairing man we had talked to before, who had rung from a bar to say that this was it. He was going under a subway, or train.

She found Dick at last in a subway station, flattened against the back wall for fear of going to the edge, and they journeyed through the treacherous hinterland south of Boston to the outlying hospital that she was told was the only place he could be admitted. Walking from the station at the end of the line, Dick knew all the junkies they passed on the street.

"I can get enough reds from any of them to kill myself."

At the hospital, he was given the brushoff in a way that made Sally feel rejected as well.

"You seem like a sane man to me," the intake worker said briskly. "All those reasons you give me for suicide would make anyone want to kill himself. You're not crazy enough for this place."

Bonded together by this humiliating experience, Sally and Dick trekked back to the center, and a medical student volunteer took him home for the night. A long time later, when Sally and I went to an Alcoholics Anonymous breakfast where Dick was to speak, he lectured us about not recognizing that drink was his main problem.

"But when we brought it up, you always said, 'I can handle it.'"

"Alcoholics always say that." Dick had become quite prim and stern now that A.A. was his life. "You should have known."

I should have known, too, that when I picked up Manuel on a street corner to take him to the treatment clinic, it was all right to let him bring his bottle in a brown paper bag; even necessary at that stage of his alcoholism. He asked me to stop at a small grocery for him to buy cigarettes. Waiting outside, I noticed that the shop sold alcohol, so I went in and stopped him from buying a little nip bottle of brandy.

Puritan fool!

"He could have gone into D.T.s before you got him here," the nurse at the detox center told me. "And you should know better than to be alone in the car."

"But I'm safe with Manny. I know him."

"You may be safe. How about him?"

I suppose we should also have known not to send one of the black volunteers to an unknown ghetto apartment, but the woman was alone and distraught and begging for help before she killed her child and then herself. When the door opened, he was greeted by her two brothers, smaller than him, but with the advantage of shotguns.

We are more prudent now, but it is not quite so exciting.

The answering service, whose night operator liked to dish out advice and good cheer to callers before he passed them on to us, was only a stop-gap to get us started. We dropped it after three months, and managed to have a volunteer in the center every night.

Before we made a rule that everyone must take a turn, there were only a few of us to do the night shifts. If someone had to cancel, it was so difficult to find another volunteer at the last minute, that I often decided to do it myself, and had to call Roy once more and say, "I can't come home."

"Can't someone else . . ."

"There's only me."

That wasn't true, but I was exhausted and monomaniac enough to think that it was. Sometimes I stayed in Boston a day and a night and most of the next day. I would tell Roy, "I'll be home by seven," because it sounded better than "I won't be home before eight," and then drive too fast and take chances.

There are two routes, inland and seaward, between Boston and North Falmouth. They are both exactly seventy miles, and they never got shorter, although I deluded myself that the road would somehow shrink or concertina, and it would not take half an hour from Neponset to the North River marshes, or from Bridgewater to the Cape Cod canal.

5

As we became better known, more people called, and came in. If the front room was busy and the sofa occupied, we sat with them on the stairs that led to the church office, or took them up into the church, to the safety of a red-cushioned pew with a door like a little pony stable, while the afternoon sun struck shafts of color through the romantic saints and angels in the Tiffany windows.

Sometimes we led them through the darkness of the basement hall to sit behind the curtains of the stage, on a tattered brocade chair and a piano stool. James, a musical volunteer used to give banjo lessons there to a deeply depressed girl who would not talk, but who would strum, with her sheltering pall of long black hair still over her face.

When she got better and could go out into society, she got pregnant by a man she met at a rock concert, but she was always grateful to the banjo teacher. Samaritans are known by their direct names and a number to distinguish them from other volunteers with the same name, so she named the baby James 108.

When the weather was warmer, we went to the ice cream parlor across the road, or to the grass bank by the lake in the Public Garden, to find seclusion among crowds. I remember a man with dead eyes, spreading pictures of his murdered child on the sticky soda fountain counter, and a thin black girl weeping silently by the lake where the swan boats glided slowly, pedaled by strong young men, while unheeding legs walked by us and children threw bits of doughnut at the ducks.

All this was better than nothing, but we had to have more space and privacy. After a few months, the church secretary led us through a basement labyrinth and, with the air of showing the bridal suite, flung open the doors of two narrow back rooms full of soot and broken baby furniture.

Crumbling concrete steps led up to a door into the alley where Brian rummaged for his coat-hangers and dead plants, one of those degenerate scuppers that run like sewers behind the old brick terraces of Boston, which front onto wide streets lined with maple trees, and glowing with magnolia in the spring.

Our own back door! We could come and go this way without disturbing volunteers on the phone, or callers sitting in the front yard. Beyond the debris in the alley, our back door looked out over a car park to the side door of the Ritz.

We scoured the rooms and painted them, and made one of them into an office and the other a place to see people, and moved in, through the alley, a sofa bed given us by Nancy's neighbor when she went to Wyoming, and a refrigerator donated by another caller, who also gave Shirley an Afghan dog, because she planned to kill herself.

We got bits of carpet, bulletin boards, beds, desks and file cabinets from the storage rooms of hospitals and insurance companies. Rabid with scrounging fever, we accepted everything offered. If we could not use it, or it was too beaten up even for us, we had only to put it out in the alley, and it would be gone overnight.

A handyman volunteer built a cubicle in the front room for the telephones, and when the church school let us have the large inner back room opposite the other two, he painted the walls and plexus of pipes under the ceiling in oranges, startling pinks and greens, and we replaced the pygmy furniture with a bright blue table long enough for a harvest feast, which we could use for meetings and training classes.

Now I had everything I needed. We could stay here forever.

Sally agreed to join me as a director about this time. Shirley, an energetic new volunteer with experience at another agency, watched our novice efforts at planning and organizing, and wanted to help. When we buzzed her on the intercom one morning and arrogantly asked her to bring coffee back to the office, she arrived with the mugs and said, "I'd like more responsibility than just carrying the coffee," so we made her a director as well.

When I first began to plan this branch of the Samaritans, I had not thought about who would run it. The social worker, Rosemary, was in charge while we were organizing. When she had to leave to take a job just before we opened, I looked around to see who would be director, and found only myself.

I had never been in control or authority over anything. I had never been in charge of anybody, except the junior nurse on Men's Surgical during the war, and she was quicker and more respectful than I, and we were both heavily controlled by Night Sister, walking the wards with a huge torch like a weapon, to see who was awake and being pampered with rationed tea.

Always in my different jobs, I had been a cog, being told what to do and how to do it, knocking off without a backward glance at knocking off time, taking risks that might get me sacked, but not risking responsibility.

I must be a natural cog. That was why I had liked being a servant, a factory hand, a nurse, a very junior reporter, a lowly volunteer with the London Samaritans, where I could be rescued from mistakes, and instructed and supervised by Chad Varah and dozens of other experienced people.

Changing from cog to drive shaft was uncomfortable. I wasn't ready for it. I did not know how to be the boss without being bossy. When I had to make decisions, I did not know when to stick to my guns in the face of disagreement, and when to be flexible and reconsider.

When I had made my first unedifying mistake as a new volunteer in London, the others had reassured me, "It can happen to anybody with their first suicide call," and given me another chance. But if my early Boston volunteers made a mistake, I was so anxious over the responsibility we had to our callers, that I jumped on them and made them as nervous as I was.

Having always before been on the side where the boss was the natural enemy, however much respected or admired, I had not realized that bitching and criticizing from below do hurt, and that harmless comments translate themselves upward as personal attacks.

Samaritans do very little bitching and no politicking, because of the kind of people they are, and the kind of organization it is, with no pinnacles of power; but I was insecure enough to get defensive over suggestions for change, or to panic if someone grumbled, with the fear that they might resign.

At meetings I would ask for complaints, and then shoot them down with "That's not true," or "You should learn how to protect yourself," if someone was airing the perennial, insoluble grumble about long-winded drunks who would not get off the telephone. So the volunteers did not say much at meetings, which forced me to talk too much, and no doubt gave them something else to grumble about; only they were too nice to tell me.

When Ruth complained that our service was no help to depressed people, and that all we were doing was putting a very small bandage over a very large wound, I knew that was not true, and yet my belief in the work tottered. Ruth was one of our best volunteers. If *she* was disillusioned . . .

It took Sally to recognize that Ruth was in a slump of depression herself, in which she could not possibly help someone else in the same unhappy state.

A few months' leave for a volunteer whose life is going wrong, and a lot of befriending from other volunteers will usually bring them back to you restored to their same enthusiasm for what Samaritans try to do. If Ruth had come back from leave and found that we had radically changed the service because of what she had felt when she was depressed, she would have been horrified.

I did not realize in those days how much care and encouragement must be given to volunteers—the lifeblood of the organization. I did not yet understand that each Samaritan has a different style on the telephone, and that if they are being sincerely themselves, it will get through to the person on the other end—not so much what is said, but how it is said.

It was much easier now that there were three of us to run the branch. Sharing the responsibility made me less anxious, and hearing the others' reactions—Sally gentle, and Shirley able to laugh—made me less critical and paranoid.

It was probably the laughter that got us through that first year of exhaustion and crises and precarious solvency, and the overwhelming amount of work created by an innocent enterprise like starting a Samaritan branch in a busy city. Samaritans who have lost their sense of humor are dead Samaritans.

It was a long journey between the front and back rooms. If the two phones in the front room were in use and the third line rang with no one in the back rooms to answer, you had to duck through a low door, down iron steps with one step missing, through the furnace room and around the looping passages to try to answer it before it stopped ringing.

In wet weather, we had basins and saucepans all over the floors, and dirty Boston water ran in from the alley down the garbage chutes. At night, a rat came out for bread crumbs under the coffee table. In July, a cloud of giant black flies descended from the skylight where the sun had hatched them, and spread through the rooms like a plague. By December, with the church's ancient heating system, the back rooms were either icy, or sizzling like a ship's boiler room.

Brian took all the shoes out of the free clothes box put out by the church, and ranged them on the wall outside in odd pairs, which he tried to sell to callers and volunteers coming and going. He and the other men still slept under newspapers in the well outside our window.

I loved the old church with its wandering passages and knocking pipes, secret rooms, and the tolerant kindness we received from the workers in the office upstairs and from the new minister who inherited us when Mwalimu was eased out for being more controversial than the draft card burners. We must have been a trial to them often, with fifty or sixty volunteers endlessly coming and going, racing around the passages, using the church hall for suppers and conferences, and with the assortment of visitors we attracted.

A young woman used to wheel her bicycle down the steps, park it in the middle of our front room, unstrap the little boy from the back seat and pull down his pants severely. This mother had made many suicide attempts and needed a lot of help. So did the child, or would in the future. When you took the mother to talk in the back room, she would have the little thing's trousers down twice before you got around the passages, and while she was talking, in jerky, dissatisfied rushes, she would jump every two minutes to inspect again with a furious face. The child was always dry. I don't know what she would have done if he had not been.

There was the man who could die at will. He had been discharged from a hospital for being all right, but he was not all right, since he had no home. When he needed a bed—a hard thing to find in Boston at six p.m. on a cold wet Saturday evening, when the Salvation Army and Pine Street shelters were full—he would go somewhere like the sofa in our front room, and make himself stop breathing.

The first time he did this, we had thought he was already dead when the rescue squad arrived and got him going again. The second time, the ambulance men said they knew him quite well, and if he came in, we should keep him sitting upright, as he could only die lying down.

One hot day an immense copper-colored man with a bare torso and a shaved polished head strode in, demanding something that we could not provide, or even understand. He pushed his way through the inner door and up the stairs to the church office to threaten an elderly helper who was stapling the parish newsletter. Sally went after him. As he shook his fist in her face, which barely came up to his chest, a wicked little curved knife sprang out from the ring on his knuckle.

"How can I help you?" she asked with a squeaky voice.

"You can buy me a beer." He looked down like an elephant surprised by a mouse.

"I'll give you a dollar not to come back again," she said, as kindly as if she were offering a child a treat.

"O.K." He clicked back the little knife before he took the dollar, and went like a huge panther out of the church door. From the sidewalk, we watched his progress far down Boylston Street by the heads turning as he slipped through the shopping crowds.

We locked the door for a day or two, but he kept the bargain. He didn't come back.

When I asked Chad whether there had ever been any violent events in the London Center, he answered mildly that he could only remember one occasion, when a man came in waving a gun, and the oldest female volunteer in the place picked up a chair and bashed it down on the back of his head.

A psychiatrist told us the safest way to behave if a man threatens you with a gun or anything else. You don't bluster or look brave. You let him see that you are as frightened as he wants you to be. You say something like "I'm really scared of you and that gun. You're very threatening and terrifying to me."

I am hoping we will never have the chance to find out if this works.

Two tall thin men in leather jackets used to slip in like black greyhounds when no one was looking. If you met them slithering around a corner, or materializing silently in a doorway, they would say they had come to volunteer. After they had been sent away with a date for an interview by a volunteer who did not know them, there would be a typewriter missing, or someone's billfold, or one of the flashlights which understudied the church's chancy wiring system. Once they went upstairs and unbolted a side door of the church, and their friends came in that night and stole some candlesticks.

Molly came in quite often to moan and sorrow about the people who had betrayed and cheated her. She was pale and grubby, perhaps younger than she looked, because she had lived on the streets and in shelters, neglected and unhealthy.

Once when she was a long time in the ladies room, I went to see if she was all right. Her dingy wig and skirt and torn sweaters were on the floor, and a young naked male was washing his underwear and himself at the basins. The same church helper who had been threatened by the man with a knife on his knuckles pottered in, and said "Excuse me," politely, and went on into one of the toilets.

Molly was not our only transvestite. We talked to many, some actual and some indulging in a fantasy of what it would be like. One of our first visitors was a shy middle-aged man in a felt hat, who wore nylon tights and a bra under his office suit, and could only be comfortable at home in a dress or a housecoat.

He had recently been transferred to his firm's Boston office, and did not know how to buy clothes. Barbara brought in a mail order catalogue and helped him to figure out sizes and styles, and order what he needed.

Grace came to us wearing a black luncheon dress with a string of good pearls and those low-heeled court shoes they still make for Boston ladies, and cast herself down sobbing uncontrollably. "Oh, help me, please help me—no one will help me," gasping and weeping and turning to water before your very eyes.

Her doctor wrote us a note to say that we should not panic or call for help, but let her cry it out. She was never cried out. After two hours of being soothed and hugged and mopped up, she would fling herself out with a wad of Kleenex to her eyes, sobbing, "No one will help me!" and you hoped she would not meet a nervous customer coming hesitantly in.

Most of our visitors were less dramatic and more helpable, and so were the people who were calling. Unhappy, confused, deeply depressed for a long time, or temporarily knocked back by life, desperate with the pain of a loss, lonely, unable to make friends, in thrall to drugs or alcohol—all day and all night, the sad or agitated or defeated voices came over the telephone, and many of them talked suicide.

People who have not been lucky enough to work in a place like the Samaritans imagine that it must be depressing to listen to so much human misery, and to be talking only to the hundreds of people who are in trouble, never to the thousands who are all right.

It is true that you sometimes find yourself looking at people on the street or in a restaurant or an airport, and wondering what sorrows and anxieties they carry, and on a subway platform, you can't help wondering why that man is standing so close to the edge; but it's not true that the work is depressing. Distressing to hear what people have to go through, and saddening often, when the story is so hopeless that there is nothing you can do but listen and share the pain, but in the long run heartening, because listening and befriending does often make a small difference, at least for the time being.

Suicide is classically called the cry for help, but it seems more like a plea for attention. Most people have not thought as far as help, but they want somebody to know how bad it is.

"Only trying to get attention," families complain about some difficult member who constantly threatens suicide, or does little desperate things like cuts or mild overdoses. But what is wrong with needing attention? We all do, but most of us can find easier ways to get it. How pitiful if a suicide attempt or threat looks to be the only way to get noticed.

Suicide prevention is not only helping people to stay alive through a crisis. It should also be like preventive medicine—helping them to avoid a crisis; trying to reach persons before things get so bad and they become so isolated that suicide seems the only thing to do.

You cannot solve the difficulty or restore the loss or change the situation, but you can at least relieve its tension. Disasters and failures given voice lose some of the menace they hold when they build up steam inside the brain, with no safety valve.

When the voice on the telephone says, "I'm going to kill myself," suicide is already a shade less likely than if the words had not been spoken. The very fact that the suicidal person has made this call, instead of pulling the trigger or downing the pills, reminds the listener that even in this crisis of despair, there is still a hope, however faint, however buried, of survival.

That is what you have to work with. Samaritans don't save lives. They try to help people to save their own lives. We don't "talk people out of it." We try to help them to talk themselves out of it.

Most people who are tempted to suicide don't really want to be dead. They want to die, because it seems the only way to escape the pain of what their life is. Hating your life is not the same as desiring death, and many suicides seem really to be accidents, because they're not completely intended.

Some of those we have tried to help do, alas, eventually kill themselves. That is hard to bear, when you have seen someone through so many nights of crisis. Why didn't they ring us this time? Why didn't they give another chance? Because then they might be still alive. Was that why they didn't ring?

There are times when it would be obtuse and insincere to try to talk to someone about living. Times when the story is so unrelievedly awful and the outlook so hopeless that you can completely understand the choice of death.

I remember a German woman alone, no family or friends to care that she was facing one more cancer operation that couldn't help much.

A man on bail and awaiting trial for something horrible, who didn't think he had a chance of avoiding a life sentence.

Dying is a lonely and secret business. That is why the call was made, and all you can do is to be someone to whom it is safe to talk about dying.

And yet, even then . . .

Sometimes it is more surprising that people don't kill themselves than that they do.

6

By the end of our second year in Boston, we had talked to about six thousand people of all ages from nine to ninety, and were getting about a hundred calls and visits each day. The work was growing far beyond what I had imagined when I said, "Let's advertise a number and see who calls."

New volunteers came to train and work with us, and some of them also left, especially in the summer, since many were college students. Sally and Shirley and I spent many hours, in that summer of 1976, filling gaps on the daytime shifts, and many extra nights in the center.

We did not mind, because we would all rather talk to callers than do finances and paperwork. My husband knew that I had to keep pace somehow with the expanding demands of what I had so modestly started, but it became no easier to ring him up and say, "I'll be late home," or "I've got to stay the night," and no easier for him to hear it. If he was angry, I felt misunderstood. If he was not angry, I felt he should be. If he was sad, I felt guilty. Although I told the volunteers that their families must come first, and not suffer because they were Samaritans, I was not following that advice myself. I knew that my daughter wanted to tell me to spend more time at home. She would start to say something, but could not finish because I did not want to hear it. I could not do it anyway—or believed I couldn't.

I had a house full of family and friends that summer, children and young people hurtling about with a lot of noise, in and out of the refrigerator, playing music, leaving trails of sand and wet towels, always in the kitchen when Roy wanted to make his lunch, with me not there to buffer the generations.

Once when I came home very late, exhausted, after two suicide emergencies and an hour's visit to a depressed, defeated man on the way home, Roy said tensely, "I know you have to do this. I know it's important. I know you're dealing with desperate people. But—well, listen . . . I have been desperate too!"

I tried to stay at home more, but in those days I still had to go to Boston three or four times a week. It was not that I felt indispensable—or was it? Having started this runaway enterprise, I felt driven to do what I saw as my share of the work.

40 Befriending

Americans talk a lot about the Protestant work ethic, but the Protestants did not invent the obsession to give your life meaning through work. Sometimes I wonder if there is not more of vanity than duty in it anyway. Would one work quite so hard if no one was looking?

Once I did not come home for six days. That was in January of 1978, when a whirling historic blizzard struck the east coast. It hit the peninsula of Cape Cod before it reached Boston, and Roy telephoned at midday, to tell me not to try to start for home. If I had, I would have been one of the thousands of drivers who ran head-on into a moving wall of snow, and had to wait in their cars for hours and even days for rescue. Some who were not found died in their cars, of cold, or of carbon monoxide poisoning if they ran the engine for warmth. Some who floundered away through the drifts were injured or died of exposure.

The lights in the church went out. The ancient furnace gave a last clank and was silent. A young volunteer, Jean, was with me, and the rest of the day and all that night, we answered the telephone by the light of candle stubs, while the snow buried the city. When we looked out into the back alley at the beginning of the night, a rampart of snow was already as high as the door, with the laden wind shrieking above it along the edge of the roofs. In the front well, it was deeper. Pressing down the steps, it shifted, and tried to fall in on us. We forced the door shut, and did not open it again.

We moved to the inner room at the back, farther away from the raging wind, under the weight of the church. We had locked the door in the passage, although we were alone in the building. After midnight, there was a knocking, insistent, deadened in the buried church, like the knocking on the inside of a coffin lid.

We looked at each other. The telephone rang. Jean grabbed it, so I had to go to the door.

I pulled the bolt and opened the door on a brightness of candle light, each flame clear and straight in the draftless air. Behind the light, the new sexton, a heavyweight woman like a boxer, held in each puncher's fist a candelabra she had brought down from the chapel.

When the candles guttered out in pools of wax on the blue table, we went back to answering the telephones in the dark. There were calls from people who were snowed in and sick, or freezing or hungry or in other states of distress, and the police had given us as one of the emergency numbers to call to get help. But the regular night litanies also came in—can't sleep, still depressed, been drinking, got to thinking, hate my mother—as if we were not all trapped in a dangerous white adventure.

To people who were toying with the idea of suicide, you had to say, in all fairness, "Not tonight. If you overdose, and then get scared and want help, I can't get an ambulance to you."

It was late morning of the next day when the endless, wind-driven snow stopped and the storm moved away to bury someone else, and the sun came out in a glaring cobalt sky. Powering a shovel, the brawny sexton dug us out like moles. Her narrow tunnel was much higher than our heads.

In the afternoon, Bill came across the river from Cambridge on skis and Chris plodded in on snowshoes, bringing raw bacon, which was all he had in his flat.

Outside, the wide streets had one cleared lane where some people slid by on cross country skis and others pulled children on toboggans, and everyone smiled and greeted each other, like an old-fashioned Christmas print. In the side streets, they trod down narrow tracks between the walls of snow which had buried the parked cars as high as the street lamps. On Beacon Hill, children in red wool hats hurtled on sleds down what used to be streets. You could hear their laughter and shrieks from far away, because there was no traffic, and no airplanes. Just the sounds of people again.

When visitors came to the center for information or on business, we were proud to be able to show them what the volunteers were doing, and hoped this would compensate for any lack of elegance. It was hardly noticeable to us, except when some smartly dressed person with an alligator briefcase had to be led through the front room, where a shopping bag lady ate doughnuts, and Molly sat with her wig and her grievance, past Frank giving his monotone recital on the stairs, "Why-don't-some-body-help-me," along the corridors, gritty with underground dirt of the ages, ducking around the drip in the bucket, stumbling over broken floor tiles, past the garbage chute, its floor a littered lake, its sink a bottomless pool of scummy gray water, past the smelly little kindergarten bathroom whose door would not stay shut, into the office with its scarred desks, where the best seat was the wicker chair from the junk shop.

Most visitors accepted it, as we did. It was cozy and unclinical, and its euphemism for shabby was "unthreatening." They understood that we were still struggling to get securely established, cutting costs whenever possible and giving most of our energies to the volunteers and the hundreds of callers they were trying to help. But one man, who was a trustee of a family foundation told us, raising his voice against the deafening twin flushes of the kiddies' bathroom in the hallway and the minister's lavabo overhead, that he might be able to grant us a sum of money, but only to help us get out of this slum.

A slum? The Arlington Street Church, with its steeple full of bells and its glorious Tiffany windows that Mwalimu had wanted to sell to pay the heating bill? What about our new white Formica coffee tables and plastic couches from the Prudential Insurance Company? Their broad tweed rug over my old kitchen carpet? The daisied wallpaper in the back room and the bright painted walls of the Sunday school room, with its ceiling decor or orange and green and salmon pink pipes?

When we finally did have to move, it was that womblike middle room where I had been buried in the snowstorm with Jean that I would miss the most. When you were in the center at night, alone or with someone else, that room felt like the hub of the world, the center of a web whose spokes were telephone lines reaching out all over the city to carry in the lonely messages.

How many nights have I lain on that hard green couch, with the telephone on the floor and the receiver jammed under my ear, listening to the unquenchable dirge of Mrs. O'Something from South Boston, who has had a couple of drinks to ease the disappointment that her husband is piggily asleep and her children never called her on Mother's Day. A good Christian woman, her trouble is that she has lived her whole life for other people with no thought for herself, and the only reason she won't kill herself is that God would send her to hell and she won't give the family that satisfaction.

The voice goes on. She does not want me to say anything, which is just as well, since by four o'clock on the morning after Mother's Day, there is a danger you might say, "I can see why they didn't send a card."

The more tired you are, the more difficult it becomes to help her to end the call. I lie on my back and trace the well-known path of the soiled pipe from the clerical bathroom, angling in at the corner, picking up a tributary from the office washroom, traveling diagonally across the low ceiling, striped red and pink and yellow to finish some cans of paint, insecurely held above my head with rusted bands. Where it disappears out by the far door, two purposeful copper pipes streak in parallel and take divergent right angled turns above my feet, one to form coils and elbow joints before it goes through the ceiling alongside a dead lead pipe with an open end, the other to slope downward to head height, with a warning Christmas bow tied at the lowest spot, and disappear into the wall through a dry sheaf of telephone wires leading nowhere, their fringed ends like sea anemones.

I remember so many of the lonely voices, the sad, the angry, the perplexed, so many lives in the balance that came into that secret place.

The young woman helplessly hooked on pain killers, who was having her teeth pulled out one by one by different dentists, to get prescriptions. The teenage prostitute who wanted, and did not want, to escape from her pimp. Georgie, who gave up her child, and wanted to take everything out of the refrigerator and shut herself inside with a can of beer. Sarah, aged twenty-nine, with the dual personality of an imaginary eight-year-old boy. When his part of her was in control, he would taunt the Sarah part to yet one more of the suicide attempts she had contracted with her therapist not to make.

Volunteers saw Sarah through many a self-destructive night. She could be diverted first by attentive love, then often by a practical suggestion, like getting up and making the spaghetti sauce for her daughter's birthday party tomorrow, instead of lying curled up on the floor between the bed and the wall, with the eight-year-old seducing her to cheat the therapist.

There were people obsessed with old useless guilts, painfully grieving, burdened with raw needs and hopeless loves they could not crawl away from, or empty with no love ever, and no knowledge of how to give or receive it.

I remember the woman who was sitting in her window, looking out at the bridge over the river, from which she would jump as soon as her ex-husband had fetched the children for the weekend. She talked a long time, at first without emotion. She was convinced of her plan. It was the obvious decision, easier for everyone. Hard on the children—briefly, they'd get over it—but better for them in the long run than this neurotic, failed mother.

And yet, she had rung us. I hung on to that, though nothing I said seemed to help. I remember saying to her at some point, as I would to a friend who was getting aggressive, "Don't bully me."

A pause. "Am I bullying you?"

"It felt like that, yes."

"My God," she said slowly. "I must have more strength than I thought."

I was aware of a tiny spark of hope, like a cinder kindled when you stir a half-burned log in last night's ashes.

We talked until she heard the children's alarm go off, and then she said goodbye. I still did not know whether she meant goodbye for now, or *goodbye*.

She had given me her number some time earlier. She said it would not matter if I tried to get in touch with her. She would not be there. I tried ringing her for several days at different times. There was no answer.

On the following Sunday she answered, breathless, a bit distracted.
"I'm just going out."
"Are you all right?"
"Yes. I'll call you."

She never did. It happens like that. You journey through a crisis with someone and then lose them, not to death, but because they have chosen life.

The family trustee did give us money, and we promised him that we would move to a new center when we could. The chairman of the British Samaritans came to visit us in 1977, and said that we should move as soon as possible. We were getting about fifty thousand calls a year. He prophesied, rightly as it now appears, that in five years' time the calls would have more than doubled.

The church had no more space to give us. Reluctantly, and with the shaky feeling of being thrown back to the beginning again, just when we were securely settled in, we began to poke about Boston for another center.

We looked at houses and some offices. They were either too small, or too depressing, or too inaccessible. Some were too daunting, ten floors up, with an armed guard in the lobby. They were all too expensive.

The agent who took us around was having a hard winter, and was in no mood for jokes. His overcoat was threadbare at the cuffs, with dandruff and brindle hairs on the rubbed velvet collar. We had to stop going around with him, because it was too hard to have to listen to his gallant recital of how a place was just what we wanted, and then turn it down.

Perhaps we would be able to stay at the church. But by now, we were not sure if wanted to. Treacherously, we had started to look at our surroundings with someone else's critical eyes.

In the spring of 1978, four years since Mwalimu Imara had given us the front room of my dreams, we found a suitable place under the vast complex of the Prudential Center, whose crown rides the sky forty-five floors up and whose foot toes the finish line of the Boston Marathon.

It was a large empty space, windowless, of course—Samaritans seem fated to live like moles—but not underground. You enter it discreetly by walking between the escalators that go up and down between the street and the raised shopping arcade, ducking under the cave of the stairs, as redolent as the well outside our window at the church, and through a heavy door into another world, as secret as the innards of the church basement.

Designed by Mardi, who was now also a director, it was cut up with inner walls to our needs—telephone room, waiting room, four little safe quiet rooms for visitors, office space, kitchen, shower.

The telephone room had soundproof walls and a sophisticated phone system, comfortable listening nooks for five or six Samaritans, and couches for two to lie down. It was clean, bright, and beautiful.

After the move in January 1979, the volunteers who had complained most about the shabbiness and inconvenience of the old center started to complain that they missed the homely coziness of the old church basement.

7

It was not until I stopped commuting to Boston almost every day that I realized what a killer it had been.

I still went in once a week, but before we moved to the new center, I had handed over the Boston branch to Shirley and Sally and Mardi, not because my energy was used up, but because founders of anything should step back before they become immovable. Also, it was time to start a second branch on Cape Cod, where I lived.

If I started a Samaritan branch in Boston to have a place to belong when I was not in London, perhaps I started the Samaritans on Cape Cod so that I would not be killed falling asleep on the highway to Boston.

A local policeman had told me that the suicide rate for Cape Cod and its southward islands, Martha's Vineyard and Nantucket, was very high. Surprising to hear, since Cape Cod is an east coast mecca, where for generations, people have been coming in the summer as children, incorporating it into their lives and recreating the magic for their children and their children's children.

Magic summers lead to the dream of one day retiring on the Cape. Those of us who do live here all the year around find that winters are less frigid than in the rest of New England, and summers are less grilling. The invasion of summer people and tourists is an endurable plague, because it is your neighbor's main source of income, and perhaps yours too. When the ravagers of summer pass on like locusts to get the children back into school after Labor Day in September, the sun and the sea water are just as warm, and the dunes and beaches are suddenly ours again. You can swim almost to the end of October.

For someone like me who lives here because I think it is the finest place in this hemisphere, it was surprising to hear the policeman talk about the high suicide rate, and to begin to discover some of the reasons why many people on Cape Cod and the Islands have fallen victims to despair.

One reason may be that rootless, dissatisfied people tend to drift here, as to any mecca, hoping to be magically healed, and then find that the sickness is here, because they brought it with them. So now what? Before they came here, they could at least think, "I could go to the Cape." Sometimes it is better not to use up that last straw idea, in case it doesn't work.

47

This may be one of the reasons for the high suicide rate in California. "Go West" used to mean a better chance for the enterprising and courageous. Now it can sometimes mean a last chance for failure and misfits. When I went to Alberta for the opening of the first Samaritan branch in Canada, I learned in this westerly province that Canadian suicides tend to increase from east to west. A pundit has also figured out something called the Land's End Syndrome, which sends the despairing to the limits of the coast, like lemmings. Cape Cod, sticking out into the Atlantic like a raised bent arm, fits that description, all right.

Some of the people who remember the summers of youth, and many for whom Cape Cod was never more than an unrealized dream, are disappointed when they return here. The husband may be demoralized anyway, the loss of belonging and purpose when he gave up his job. The wife, even if she has not lost a job, has lost her house and its neighborhood to which she has belonged, the friends she knows, and the society where she is known.

It is not so easy to meet new people when you are middle aged. Friends and family may visit in the summer, but in the winter, you're on your own. The summer colony in which you bought or built a house turns out to be a desert of empty cottages and closed shops. Where is everyone? What is there to do? At home—even after several years, you still think of the place you have sold as home—you never used to drink before six. Exiled to the Cape, drinks began to be needed earlier.

Alcohol and suicide are closely linked, and the authorities say that Cape Cod and the Islands have the second highest rate of alcoholism in the United States. They never tell you which place is first, and no doubt there are a hundred other places claiming to be second, but it is obvious that Cape Cod, which is popularly known as a strip of sand held together by bars and liquor stores, is right up there competing.

There are not enough jobs for local people. Not much in the winter, and in the summer, when the population more than triples, the waitress and barman and chambermaid jobs go to the bright and beautiful college students who pour over the bridges to finance a summer here.

Children who grow up in the Cape are lucky, but if they don't get off it when they leave school, they may get stuck. They marry the school-days lover, or move in together, have babies, have no jobs, go on welfare, hunt in vain for a house to lease that they won't get thrown out of at the end of May when the rents rocket up for the summer.

And then the bridges. . . . There are two of them, four miles apart at each end of the Cape Cod canal. They soar in spectacular arcs, high enough for big ships to pass under, high enough to kill you if you jump. The railings were built at waist height, which has made it tempting and easy.

The bridges were built in 1933. Since police started to keep records in 1963, about sixty people have jumped to their deaths. Peanuts compared to the score of seven hundred from the Golden Gate bridge across San Francisco Bay, but still some sixty people who might be alive today if the canal bridges had not offered the handy temptation to act on a suicidal impulse.

It often happens in life that when you get one shove, you soon get another in the same direction, in case you might fancy that you could avoid your destiny.

Just after I had talked to the policeman who knew about suicide, a woman rang me from a nearby town. She said that the Samaritans had saved her life in Scotland, and when it needed saving again on Cape Cod, the agency she called hung up on her because she was drunk, without waiting to hear that she was asking for help to stop getting drunk.

She took me to see the young minister at Woods Hole, who had helped her, and before I knew it, we were off again with steering committee, fund raising, a public meeting, newspapers, volunteers coming hesitantly forward, "I don't know if I'd be any use. . . ."

Those are the ones you want. The ones who come with a bold eye and a conviction that they are just what you want should not even get into the training class.

Once you have one branch going, it is easier to start the next. The Samaritans were already somewhat known, so I did not have to spend a lot of time explaining. Nor did I get nonplused by anyone objecting, "Why do we need this?" I knew by now that wherever there are people, there is a need for someone to talk to.

Boston volunteers came down to help with interviewing and training, and when we had our first little group of twenty-five, they could go to the Boston center to get some experience before we opened.

Being Cape Codders, many of them behaved like Islanders, as hard to shift as the cagey population of Martha's Vineyard and Nantucket. To go over the canal bridges to the foreign country of the mainland was a major enterprise, and if I wanted them all to go to Boston, I had to take many of them myself.

I still spent a lot of time in the Boston center, and now I was there about two nights a month with a volunteer from the Cape, watching them gain confidence and learn from the callers, enjoying their discovery—however careful the training, volunteers essentially have to make it for themselves. Listening is better than talking. Bright ideas, wise comments and easy solutions are irrelevant interruptions.

Many of the regular callers I had come to know so well since 1974 were still telling the same tale. Saddening to see that they had taken no steps away from the doldrums or the grievance or the paralysis of will or desire. We worry that, like an alcoholic's wife, who, with patient loyalty and camouflage enables him to go on drinking, our befriending might merely enable people to go on being what the Australians call the No Hopers.

If we seem to be only maintaining rather than helping, we do continue to explain to long-time callers that they need more expert help than we can give, and that we don't want to keep them from getting it by making it too easy for them to stay miserable.

Suggesting that people should not continue with endless, circular calls is one thing. Getting them to stop is another. Anyone can ring us at any time for any reason, and just because we feel that someone should be weaned does not mean that they agree.

Who says we're not helping them? We do, not they. There was a dog once who objected, "Who made up the rule that dogs should only be fed once a day? They never asked *me*."

Face it. Veteran complainers with the needle stuck in the groove can be boring. They challenge patience. They won't "get better." They make volunteers feel inadequate.

That's why they have no one but us to talk to. And who are we there for anyway—ourselves, or the caller?

The same old sex callers were also still ringing, with the same old stories. Masturbation fantasies are low on variety, and tend to stick to incest, window watching, big black men in bed with my wife, just had my first homosexual experience. The same men try all the agencies, anywhere a number is advertised. When we opened the Cape Cod branch, some of the old Boston friends started to ring us there, with the same stories.

You get to know the voice, usually pleasant and articulate, although the name may change. When the telephone is answered by a new volunteer who does not know the voice or the story, it is a fair bonus for these persevering callers. If there is a sex caller's grapevine, it starts to throb when a new class has been trained: "Ring 'em now!"

My friend Sarah, the spaghetti sauce maker with the double personality, was still in contact, and I often went to see her when I was in Boston. She had been struggling since childhood with the malevolent, seductive little fantasy boy she had created during a crisis, when she imagined herself betrayed and deserted by her parents.

They had sent her unwillingly to a summer camp when she was eight, and when she first told me the pitiful story, I was tugged painfully back to the memory of my own daughter, Pam, whom we had sent briefly to a camp at about the same age.

Shy Pam, my shadow, went for two weeks to the riding camp near our village, in the woods by the shore of New Silver Beach. There were horses at home, but she was afraid, and it was thought that she might learn not only to ride on safe camp ponies, but to become less dependent on me.

I took her to the camp on a Friday and delivered her to a merry girl counselor with thick tow[-headed] hair and muscular bare thighs, who was in charge of Pam's cabin.

"When can I visit?"

"Not till next weekend."

"I only live two miles away. Can't I just . . . I mean—see how she's getting on with her riding? She might . . ."

"Let her settle down with us."

Pam was in the cabin, sitting woefully on her suitcase.

One of the paths where we rode ran alongside the camp, past their fenced ring and broken-down, homey stable where the ponies were tended worshipfully by the little girls who had left comfortable homes all over New England to dwell in squalor in the dilapidated cabins in the damp woods.

I rode down that path the next day, pretending not to look for Pam. She was not near the stables, but far away by the marsh at the back of the dunes a crowd of shrieking girls milled about at some game with a ball. Standing apart, a square figure in a red jacket could have been Pam.

It rained. She had not taken her rubber boots. On Sunday, I parked outside the church, and when I saw her come out with a crowd of little ones who made the healthy counselors look oversized, I rushed over with the boots.

"You didn't," Roy said when I came home. "You didn't take the boots to the church."

"I had to."

"What happened?"

"She screamed and hung onto my clothes. They pulled her away and told me, 'Go Home,' as if I were a wandering dog."

That evening, I rang Miss Bea, who was in charge of the camp, at her log-built cottage which was only slightly larger than the soggy Lilliputian cabins.

"I'd better come and fetch her tomorrow."

"Why? She's adjusting beautifully. She rose to the trot this afternoon."

"This morning she cried, and begged, 'Take me home.'"

"The campers would be just fine if the parents would leave them alone."

Easy for her to say. Fairly easy for me to accept at the time, ruefully, and re-tell immediately as a joke against myself.

But not so easy to ferret out in retrospect an understanding of which is worse for the child—"better" is not the right word. Abandonment to her own resources? A tug-of-war between the old safe world and the new adventure? The cowardly reluctance of a parent to let go?

You must let go, of course, for the sake of the child's future, but who can guess at the pain and misinterpretation of the present?

My friend Sarah had been sent to a lakeside summer camp because her parents were going on a Caribbean cruise. They were taking her older sister, and Sarah thought she was only being left behind because she was afraid of water and had not learned to swim. They would visit the camp to say goodbye before they sailed, and she believed that if she could swim by then, they would take her too.

After a giant and agonizing effort, she conquered her terror of the lake, and learned to swim in two weeks. Her parents came, and before they left, she plunged into the water and swam farther out than ever before to show that she could reach the diving raft.

It was time for them to leave. They waved and called, but the skinny little body that never tanned still sat on the raft, trying to muster courage for the swim back.

"We have to go," her father said. "We have a plane to catch."

"She's having a good time out there," a counselor said easily. "Why not just go? It will be easier for her."

When Sarah somehow made the heroic effort of slipping from the raft into the water, and struggled back to shore more dead than alive to receive the praise of her parents, they had gone.

Sarah spent the rest of her weeks at camp mostly off in the woods by herself. To fill the black hole left by what she saw as deceit and desertion, she created an eight-year-old boy called Jonathan to comfort her.

When her parents returned and she went back to school, the boy was too much a part of her to banish. She seemed all right, but her daydreaming was taking her out of reach. The eight-year-old boy was becoming dominant, and it was increasingly difficult to conceal him from everyone else. That was when she made her first suicide attempt, partly to escape Jonathan, partly to escape his discovery.

She swallowed insect poison from the cupboard under the sink. She threw most of it up, and was treated at the hospital for accidental poisoning.

Eighteen years and several suicide attempts later when I first met her at the Samaritans, with her marriage broken and her husband trying to have the children taken away from her, the boy playmate was still with her, and still eight years old.

You could see her slip into his personality before your very eyes. If she was frustrated and confused, or annoyed with your refusal to let her do something like setting fire to the waste paper basket "to get the anger out"—a currently fashionable therapeutic phrase—she would sit with knees apart and small feet planted, face plump, sullen, making a small boy's stubborn mouth and blanked out eyes. Once, as Jonathan, she jumped up and ran out of the back room, around the corridors, through the front room and out of the door. Tearing after her, I found her in the middle of the empty Sunday street, standing defiantly for nonexistent traffic to run her down.

She usually called us when the suicidal fit was on her, but sometimes she did not call for help until after she had cut herself or swallowed too many pills, of which she had a variety and abundance.

She had been in many hospitals. I visited her in one of them, to which she had been admitted after quite a large overdose.

This was a Bedlam type of Victorian prison, the only place that would take her, since she had worn out her welcome at the psychiatric units of other Boston hospitals by the destructive games she could not help. Cigarette burns and cuttings—her arms were scarred from wrist to shoulder. She always wore long sleeves, except when showing off— minor fires, razor blades slipped into cigarette packages, pills collected for an orgy. Once she had hung herself from a clothes hook with a lamp cord; the doors of both the cupboard and the room wide open to insure rescue.

The hospital lobby was empty, cold, and cheerless. No one was at the desk. I followed signs along corridors, and stood back at a narrow corner for a procession to pass. A leggy, bearded man carrying a beach ball walked bouncily in shorts and gym shoes, leading a line of patients. The first one, a teenager with no teeth, had his hands on the waistband of the leader's shorts. Each of the others had a hand on the waist of the one in front, as if they were newly blind. The last woman was crying.

I found Sarah in the third floor day room. It was a square bare room with a tattered sofa and a few lopsided armchairs, two lines of metal chairs facing each other down the middle, and a table by the window where a woman and a man sat with their heads buried in their arms. There were more people than chairs. A few patients sat on the floor. Some paced, following individual tracks between fixed points, with detours around furniture and each other. In an office at the side, two women sat on the desk and talked to a man who leaned back in the swivel chair with his feet on the desk between them. In front of the main door, two huge female sentries sat with arms crossed over powerful chests.

Sarah was sitting on a ledge by the wall with her feet drawn up. She never sat with her short legs crossed or dangling, always with her feet tucked under her. She was pale, and her eyes looked dark and hectic. Beside her was the canvas satchel she took everywhere, with her journal, poems, and creased papers in it.

"What a ghastly place."

"It's worse for you than for me," she said. "I've always been here before. You should see the Quiet Room."

"What's that?"

"Solitary. No window. No door handle. No furniture. No light switch. No light, if the aide doesn't feel like turning it on."

"Why were you there?"

"I freaked out. Went crazy. Something to do."

I sat beside her. While we talked and looked at her poems, people came coming up to ask questions, or show us something, or to stare. One man came to shake my hand and remind me, stammering, that we had met in the basement room at the Arlington Street Church. Sarah was distressingly at ease in this uneasy room. She knew who to answer kindly, who to ignore, who to tell, "Fuck off, Jack. I've told you before."

When I left, one of the sentries heaved herself up to open the door. Instantly, a girl with long tangled hair made a bolt for it. The woman shoved Sarah and me back into the room with the flat of her hand, and locked the door. The lift gates clanged. Bells rang in the corridor. The man in the office did not take his feet off the desk. One of the women looked out of the doorway, then drew back her head and went on talking.

"What excitement," I said.

Sarah shrugged. "Something to do. She's not going anywhere."

Some months after the visit to the hospital, Sarah stumbled on the steps to the church basement, distraught and shivering. Her children were in a foster home. The doctor whom she saw three times a week was out of town. Sarah had often threatened to kill herself when the doctor was away. This time she was not saying, "I'm going to do it." Wrapped in a blanket, her waxen face shrunk to child size, she was saying through chattering teeth, "I have to do it!"

"Suicide is an angry, panicky, uncontrollable gesture which appears forced upon you. There is no alternative—it must be done!"

Sarah had written that in a calmer time. *It must be done.* That was how she felt.

She wanted to go back to the hospital. They had agreed to readmit her if necessary, so I took her there.

It was a Sunday. A few people were sitting in the bleak lobby. They looked as if they had been there for a long time. There was no intake worker on duty. Sarah was told she would have to wait.

We waited four hours. Twice Sarah went to be sick in the ladies' room. The third time, she was sick into the cigarette stubs in a metal ashtray on a stand.

At first, I sat on the hard couch with my arm around her, but she shrugged away. When I held her hand, she took that away and put it in the pocket of the reefer jacket she wore over her faded jeans. Teenagers clothes. At thirty, she wore them to be as different as possible from the Jewish American Princess she imagined her parents wanted her to be. They didn't, but it was easier for her to think so.

We did not talk. She was remote from me.

"Is Jonathan with you?" Her lower lip was poked out, like the eight-year-old.

She did not nod, but her eyes slid sideways at me, with Jonathan's recalcitrance. I thought of one of the poems she had shown me, in which she had asked him:

> Do you know what mate
> We're all alone now. . . .
> But why does your side drag so
> Upon my need? . . .
> Why forever must you deplete
> The source from which you spring. . . ?

When a busy, preoccupied person came for her, she got up and walked away, hunched very small in the navy jacket, without saying goodbye or looking back.

When her doctor returned, Sarah left the hospital, and things seemed to improve. Jonathan went underground. She still called us from time to time if he surfaced, or if she needed reassurance, and talked about different things with different volunteers.

Sometimes she used another name, hoping not to be recognized. She wanted to be someone who had never called us before, and to tell any version of her story she chose.

The next time I saw her in that hospital, she was a day patient, free to meet me in the lobby, which looked much brighter, because she did.

We went to the cafeteria, and Sarah took the papers out of her canvas satchel and spread them out for me on the greasy, coffee-ringed table. There were neatly typed poems, letters to her parents and children and to that lover-child Jonathan, bits of her journal, and some disorganized cries of agony, stabbed onto the creased pages in big letters, a few words askew down the page.

"Psychotic writing." She grinned sideways, to see if I was impressed.

As she showed me some of what she had written over the years of her illness, her eyes were alive, not hectic, but shining with genuine creative pleasure. She laughed a lot, and told me shocking stories about the hospital. People at other tables stared glumly. Sarah nudged me and giggled and whispered behind her hand. We were like two teenagers in a snack bar, us and them, secure in our own nutshell.

It was soon after her stay at the hospital that Sarah got her daughters back from the foster home where they had stayed after her last suicide attempt. Her therapy was going well. She had enrolled in a college course, and her parents, who continued to support her, had set her up in a comfortable apartment, where she and the girls took care of each other. I used to go and have tea with them on my way home to Cape Cod.

Sometimes we sat in her bedroom, because that was where the record player was, and she liked to play her special song about unicorns to me. She would lie on the bed and the little girls would be in and out, jumping on and off the bed, snuggling, clambering all over her, joining in the conversation before they ran out again. Sarah never changed the subject when they came in. Everything was discussed with them— freaking out, suicide, borderline psychosis, their father's intermittent attempts to get custody.

They were intelligent children with serious maternal faces, from having had to mother their mother through many bad times. Whatever the long term effects for them, the apartment was a nest of closeness for all three, with Sarah, now that she was no longer knotted into a ball of despair, inventive, amusing and tender with Sue and Amy.

"The social worker didn't want us to come back yet," Sue told me with the knowledgeable candor of an old campaigner. "But this time they let me and Amy choose."

Although the destructive alter ego was still hovering within reach, Sarah's therapist had helped her to develop a third character, level-headed Jean, who was a safer alternative than the demonic small boy when she needed to escape into another person. She and Jean, who had some orderly habits, were working on a book about Sarah's experiences in mental hospitals. It was taking shape out of the journals and poems and scrawled pages that she had shown me in the hospital cafeteria.

I went to Australia, and when I came back after several months, Nancy, the young Samaritan who had also made close friends with Sarah, told me that she was now living in a halfway house.

It was a cramped little shingled house in one of those shabby streets on the far western edge of Boston. To reach it you had to follow Commonwealth Avenue for miles while it deteriorates into used car lots and boarded-up delicatessens before it emerges, like a diver coming out of the water, into the trees and lawns and prissy dwarf evergreens of the suburbs.

Eight or ten people were jumbled contentedly into the small house. Sarah shared a ground floor room. We sat on the bed, because the only chair had clothes and books on it, and she talked about Sue and Amy who were back in the foster home, not with anguish but rather nostalgically, as if she accepted the need for someone else to take care of them now. She talked about their visits to this house, and showed me a picture of them sitting on the front step with their hair pinned up and their feet in the weedy garden.

"Sometimes we go to the movies, or get ice cream. Then I take them home on the bus," she said, almost with a note of relief, as if she were their grandmother.

She took me into the kitchen for coffee. The young man in charge of the house, who had a soft, tawny beard and a hollow waist under a long apron, and a nice air of being in the same boat as everyone else here, was preparing some kind of rice dish that involved much precise chopping of left-over turkey, apples, onions, and celery.

"You've made too much again." Sarah stirred at the huge bowl with a fork, and tasted. "What happened to the rest of the beef stroganoff?"

The young man made a face. "I'll have to throw it out."

The men and women who lived in the house wandered in and out of the kitchen to meet me, and tell Sarah things, or ask her advice. She seemed to be the leading spirit of this community, whose members were mostly on their way between a hospital and the outside world. She was not only more confident than they were, but more confident than I had seen her for a long time.

When she lived in the apartment with the children, a lot of her confidence had come from them. "Let's see what Amy thinks." "Sue, I need to go and buy oranges. Will you come with me?"

She had come here after some kind of breakdown, during which she had, among other things, stood in the street outside the apartment and tried to get run down by a bicycle. She had not brought this confidence to the house. It had come from the others here, from finding herself the one-eyed man in the country of the blind.

When I left the halfway house, with the stroganoff heavy and clammy in a plastic bag for the dogs, I felt hopeful about Sarah's life. After several months, her energy and courage had increased so much that she was able to join a campaign for the rights of mental patients. She was to interview city politicians, so she came into the Samaritan center to see if a volunteer would go to the first interview with her. She was wearing a wide-brimmed green porkpie hat like a woman at a dog show, and seemed so well-knit and cheery that I was surprised that she was still in the halfway house.

One morning not very long after that, I came up to Boston for a meeting. Shirley met me at the door, and said right away, "Something bad has happened."

"Someone died." I knew that, from her face. We had been through it with a few of the people we had tried to help. It doesn't get easier.

"Sarah."

Her doctor, loved and depended on, "the sun and moon of my days," who had stuck by her through four years of Sarah's intermittent attempts to be rejected, had gone abroad. After a good time out of sight in the world of the functioning, Sarah was once more acceptable to one of the classier Boston hospitals she had successfully outraged. They had agreed that if she felt suicidal while her therapist was away, she could be admitted to their psychiatric unit.

She had felt suicidal—she often did when the doctor was beyond telephone reach—and she had gone to the emergency room and got herself admitted, to be safe. After two days of being watched, she found a way to leave the building, and went back to the halfway house to get some clothes. She came into the Samaritan center, very agitated, and agreed with the volunteer who saw her that she should go back to the hospital. She left distraught, running out before anyone could go with her.

On suicide precautions at the hospital, she was supposed to have a nurse with her at all times, or to be checked every fifteen minutes when she was asleep, and touched under the bedclothes, to make sure she had not cut herself or taken pills.

Yesterday evening, she had told the nurse she wanted to sleep.

"You don't have to sit there," she said. "It annoys me. I'm all right. Please leave me alone for a bit."

The nurse went away for fifteen minutes, was called to do something, got involved and did not come back for two hours. She found Sarah hanging in the cupboard with a lamp cord around the clothes railing. She had not left the door of the room open this time, presumably because she felt certain the nurse would come back.

And yet, who knows? After so many indecisive attempts, so much flirting with death, who knows when the time will come to decide, "This is it?"

A last scrappy poem, disordered by the drugs they were giving her, was found in her bag in the hospital room.

> It it it—nameless throbbing that is there
> How can I surpass you?
> It hurts. I try.
> We fall again—dismal.
> . . . .
> What can I do now?
> Give me a measure of strength.
> I can survive but alone.
> I want, I even do, I know. I try,
> But fool me always—I hurt. I hate. I won't.
> *HOLD ME NOW!*"

"I hate." I won't suggest the alter ego Jonathan, emperor of his own destruction.

I still could not feel that she had truly meant to be dead this time. Nor did her parents. I met them for the first time, since Sarah had always wanted to keep the different people in her life separate. Sue and Amy wandered in and out of the family's motel rooms, quite controlled, very docile. They wrote a story about what death was like for their mother—being free, giving up smoking—which was read at the memorial service.

Almost half the gathering were either Samaritans or fellow patients. The young man who made risotto and stroganoff came with the whole population of the halfway house, looking scared. I also recognized the girl with the long hair who had bolted for the door at the Bedlam hospital, and from another hospital a roommate whom Sarah used to bring into the center, where I could sit and listen to them amicably chipping away at each other, "Don't play those psychotic little games. I know them all."

A week later, Sally and I were asked to go to the halfway house to talk about Sarah. It was very hard. We crowded into an upstairs room, sour with cigarette smoke. Everybody spoke about the last time they had talked to her, and again it was clear that they had counted on her to be the most stable one in the house. . . . A young man shook, and wept uncontrollably, not so much for Sarah, as for his own frailty. If she could not survive, how could he?

It is a terrible experience to lose somebody you have tried to help and have grown to love, especially when you feel sure that they did not completely mean to be dead. No—losing somebody is the wrong expression, because they never belonged to you. The death does not affect your life, like the loss of someone in the family, or a very close friend, but it affects your thinking for a long time.

You have to try to dispose of guilt—and then not to feel guilty about not feeling guilty, so insidiously does guilt come in at the cracks—because all along one of the premises of your helping is that the other person is free to do what they want. Even to die, if that is what they really desire.

But it still hits you powerfully as a mistake, a tragic waste, not only of the person and the life they have not yet lived, but of the pain and struggle you have watched them go through. The other words, the ones that toll for any death, are: Too Late. Even if you honestly think you have done the best you can, you have never done enough.

The memorial to a suicide can only be the rueful hope of doing more and better for the next person.

Sometimes people cannot be helped to live, but they may need to talk about their dying, and it may be easier to do it with a stranger. Family reactions to terminal illness range anywhere from ignoring the truth or refusing to talk about it, to being so adult and well-informed about Death and Dying—now an educational category in its own right—that they can talk of nothing else.

I remember a man telling me once, "I probably have a few more months. But they've read all the books and attended all the classes, and they're all so well prepared for my death that I feel out of place, being still alive."

A young man called Bobby rang us almost every day for months to talk about his terminal cancer, and the diminishing days of his life. He lived in a town near Boston, where Rebecca, a young volunteer went to visit him, then went off by himself to a cottage in Maine, because he wanted to be alone.

He still telephoned us from there, reversing the charges from two hundred miles away, and talked in a light, calm voice about death and what came after, and about pain, and the small change of his enclosed, self-absorbed life. Rebecca and I kept close to him on the telephone, and dreaded the day that he would die.

During this time, when we knew Bobby did not have very long, we were persuaded by a psychotherapist we knew to attend a group sensitivity session that she said would make us better Samaritans. Ten or twelve of us risked it. On an upstairs floor of a late Victorian house in Brookline, we sat on a bedroom carpet blindfolded, and were led one by one into the therapy chamber, where we were ordered to lie on our backs on the floor and kick our legs and feel like babies.

I did not feel like a baby. I felt like a middle-aged woman who has gotten herself into something she can't get out of. After we were allowed to crawl unblinkered, and then to grow up and sit on chairs, we went through several reasonably humiliating exercises, role plays and confessions, which may have made us more sensitive, but not in the way we had hoped for.

We were told to go over to somebody and thank them for something. The therapist's assistant crawled over to where the therapist sat cross-legged on the floor, laid his square beard on her tights and thanked her for allowing him to do this work. I moved in a bleary trance across the room to Rebecca, and kneeling down, laid my maudlin head in her lap and thanked her for sharing the sorrow of Bobby with me. She leaned her long silken hair over me, and she wept too.

Afterwards, when we got our egos back, we all felt worse, not better, for losing control. If we could be tricked into losing our grip on our own emotions, how were we going to help anybody else? How was this going to help Bobby?

After that, Rebecca and I avoided each other, and did not exchange notes on the news from Maine, until she got a call one weekend from Bobby's father. Although he had not met her, he knew that his son was her friend. He was telephoning now, alas, to tell her that Bobby had died.

"I felt so bad for him," Rebecca told me. "He sounded like an older Bobby. He said, 'My poor son,' and cried a bit."

We were sad, but not surprised. In the last few weeks, the calls had been getting shorter, and Bobby's voice more fatigued. We wrote to the parents, and sent flowers. There was no acknowledgment.

Weeks later, Rebecca pulled into a gas station. As she stopped her car by the pumps, a young man came briskly out of the office, got into a car and drove away. It was Bobby.

I resented even more the babyish, facile tears at the psychotherapist's house. I felt betrayed—but not by Bobby.

If announcing his own death was the only way he could get rid of Rebecca and me, good luck to him. So what if he never had cancer at all? Who is to say that the effort and emotion—the honest, not the artificial emotion—we had spent on him was wasted? If it supplied something he needed, did it matter if the need was not his dying, but something else we did not know about?

Some people do use the Samaritans to try out their dreams as reality. An improbable voice will tell you of being a powerful executive, or pursued by three women, or close to the President. A shy young girl will tender alarming tales of incest, battering, rape, leukemia or dramas of romance and peril.

Does it matter what's true and what's invented? The fantasy may be a necessary weapon of survival. We cannot do much about the ennui and emptiness out of which it is spun, but we can at least provide the attention the soul of the spinner craves.

8

The Samaritan branch on Cape Cod was started, like London and Boston and many other branches, in the basement of a church.

The Samaritans are not religious. The name was used in a newspaper headline when Chad Varah first started it in 1953, and it stuck. The volunteers, like callers, are of all faiths or none, and the concept of listening and befriending seems to fill a need everywhere, all over the world, whatever the style of the local deity.

Churches, however, often have space and generosity, and are usually glad to share in Samaritan work. Some ministers, seminarians and nuns are Samaritans in mufti. I remember Sister Catherine in a cotton dress and headscarf sitting tranquilly with a man in the Arlington Street basement, listening to his true story of violence and banditry. When it was time for her to return to the convent, another volunteer took over, and Catherine reappeared from the ladies' room in her dark flowing habit and broad-winged coif. The man's eyes followed this large bird through the room with stunned mistrust. He had no idea that it was Catherine.

St. Barnabas Church in the old part of Falmouth, where the square white clapboard houses with black shutters surround the village green, gave us a tiny underground room, about six by eight, where the choirboys used to change and scrap about.

You reached it through the vestry door. At the bottom of a steep narrow stair was our mole-hole telephone room, with a convertible sofa from a motel that exactly filled the floor space when pulled out to make a bed. And yes, there was a network of pipes under the ceiling to look at you as you lay listening to the litany of the good Christian woman who has lived all her life for others who don't appreciate her, which can be heard on Cape Cod as well as in Boston, or anywhere else you choose to provide an ear.

There was a small nook to make coffee, and a little cave under the arch of the stairs, where we put two chairs for people who came in to talk. If they came on Sundays, or Saturdays in wedding season, they had to talk loud, because of the organ and hymns above.

The telephone company would not run a line into the church. They left a coil of gray wire at the foot of a distant pole, and my daughter and her husband and I spent a cold wet Saturday digging a deep trench across fifty yards of church lawn. When a wedding party came out under umbrellas, we saluted them, like grave diggers.

We laid in the wire, stamped back the earth and sods of turf, and by November 2, 1977, the telephone was connected. This was the twenty-fourth anniversary of the modest debut of the Samaritans in St. Stephens, Walbrook in London, and perhaps no subsequent branch has ever opened more modestly than in our little burrow under St. Barnabas Church; Falmouth, Massachusetts.

When we started the Boston branch, the telephone rang almost at once. On Cape Cod, we hardly got any calls at first, except from people who hung up as soon as we answered, or pretended that it was the wrong number, because they were testing to see how we sounded.

The volunteers patiently came and went, and read or studied or knitted or dozed, and I ran about the neighborhood like a mad cockroach, trying to find more ways to make us known. The volunteers were calm, but I was panicky. Perhaps we were not needed. Perhaps the people were right who complained, "Why do you need a suicide prevention service in a paradise like Cape Cod?"

The local newspaper editor reassured us. "Of course you're needed. The Samaritans are needed everywhere, but it will take the Cape Codders a year to accept you."

In country places like this, it is not only that there are fewer people, but those who need you are more suspicious than city dwellers of something new, and more afraid of gossip. However careful you are to keep everything confidential, including who the Samaritans are, it takes time for people to feel safe. It did not take a year, but it took several months for the Cape Codders to trust us, and for the calls and visits to begin, and for the need to talk to show itself here, as anywhere else.

Because we had more time than the Boston branch, we were able to send out volunteers more often to see people who could not come to us. Most country places in "progressive old America" have no local buses or trains, but there are still many people who have no car, or who don't drive, or wouldn't drive farther than the nearest shops and post office. There is no mail delivery either.

Volunteers went, as they do now five years later, to lonely old ladies in one-room apartments where you step in the cat bowls; to young mothers who can't cope with babies; to suicidal men in police lockups; to women who are afraid a husband won't come back—or afraid that he will.

John drove to an empty car park by a frozen beach. The middle-aged man, sitting in his car staring at the rough ice on the edge of the sea, couldn't cope with retirement.

"We planned it all. We came here summers. I spent thousands of dollars putting in heat and a garage. She loves it. I'm bored. I'm nobody. There's nowhere I've *got* to go, so I go nowhere. I'm drinking. God." He turned his head to look at John properly in the dusk. "You're only half my age. What can you know?"

But difference in age hardly ever seems to matter. Sometimes it is even an advantage. If the volunteer is the age of your children, with whom you don't talk easily, it can be an encouraging discovery to find yourself talking candidly and closely. If you're a teenager, you may think you can't talk to someone older, until you find you can. You're being listened to and taken seriously by someone you always thought of as the enemy.

John and the retired businessman were together many times, and the talking helped to bridge the gap between the old life and the new. He eventually got involved in a tutoring program, which John had casually suggested, careful not to push it, because you can make people worse by urging solutions on them so enthusiastically that they feel guilty for disappointing you if they can't do that.

A young man in Boston who had dropped out of college for a depressed two years, called one day to tell me that he had registered again for September.

"Fantastic!" I cried. "That's wonderful, Donald. I'm proud of you."

A quite new volunteer was listening. When I had finished carrying on, she asked me, "What happens if he changes his mind? How will he be able to tell you?"

Kay went to find a girl who had cut her wrists feebly in the woods behind her school. Ted spent a day in court with a runaway from a foster home. I spent a night in a hospital emergency room with Jill, who had taken her boyfriend's pills.

She sounded all right, but shaky. She obviously needed help, but refused to let me send for an ambulance, or to tell me where she was.

She finally agreed to let me come, but not to the house. I found her tottering down a side road in the rain in very high heels, satin disco pants and sleeveless pink top, shivering and afraid.

"I thought it would make him sorry for me." She sat in the car like a thin stray cat. "But as soon as I'd taken them, I knew it would make him more angry."

I had planned to call an ambulance after I reached her, but she seemed well enough to drive with me to the hospital.

There were two ambulances already at the emergency entrance, delivering car crash victims. Jill and I were put into a curtained cubicle. Through a gap at the end, I could see and hear the car crash man and woman on beds in the middle of the room, not badly hurt, and their two chums making drunken jokes, as if ending up in a hospital with a few cuts about the face and head was a hilarious way to round off an evening's fun.

A young doctor gave them all a few pieces of his mind, and I could hear them start to giggle again about it as he came briskly into our cubicle. Jill sat upright on the high bed, with her thin hair sticking out at odd angles, her Adam's apple working, as if she would throw up before the nurse brought the ipecac.

While she was vomiting up her soul into the basin on her knees, a social worker came and leaned nattily on the side rail of the bed and fired questions at her like rivets.

Jill tried to answer, but I had to finish for her, as much as I knew.

"Her parents are in North Carolina. She isn't going to give you their telephone number. Telling them is the worst thing she can think of."

When Jill was emptied of what appeared to be all her body fluids, the doctor came back with a plastic cup of pitch black liquid with a scum on top, like those noxious ponds found in hollow places at the dump.

"If some of the pills have gone beyond your stomach, this will get rid of them in the other direction."

"Diarrhea?" Jill turned up her red eyes, with her ashen face still bent down.

"You got it." He held the cup to her mouth. "It tastes vile, so drink it all at once."

"Wait a minute." She pushed his hand aside. "Will it—I mean, it works quickly?"

"Quicker the better."

"Because," she said practically, a smear of the black stuff clownish on the remains of her lipstick, "I've got leotards on. I can't get them off in a hurry."

"Look kid," he said, "you should have thought of that before you took the pills."

It was not so much the unkindness, as the monstrous unreason of it that floored Jill and me. We took the terrible charcoal drink to the ladies' room and she drank it there, and we left without seeing the doctor again.

I suppose he was having a bad night, although the cut faces were asleep and their drunken friends sent home, and there was nothing much else doing but a foot cut on broken glass at a beach party. But the chatter about the leotards had done him in.

With some notable exceptions, people who make small suicide attempts get short emotional shrift in emergency rooms.

They are tended to physically, but in the average busy hospital, no one, understandably, has time for much more than a brief, "Why did you do it?"

A psychiatrist may be available, but only after a long wait, and usually not at nights and weekends, which is when most dramatic events seem to happen. When the hapless attempter has been emeticked or pumped out or bound up, they are often discharged alone, perhaps with a note of the telephone number of the mental health clinic.

"Which they aren't going to call," emergency room nurses agree. They worry about people like Jill, knowing that they can't supply more than their physical needs. They worry about the repeaters, knowing that more time and attention might make it less necessary for them to come back again and again.

But suppose you have spent the last three or four hours working flat out with heart attacks, injured children, burned firemen—innocent victims. You haven't much left over for poor old Blanche coming in for the fourth or fifth time with a towel around her wrist. You may even feel angry with Blanche, and then later you feel guilty about being angry.

Once in Boston, I took a distraught man to the emergency psychiatric department of one of the city hospitals. They took his name and some details, looked at the superficial cuts he had made on his cheek with a beer bottle cap, and left him and me to sit endlessly in the waiting room. A top-heavy woman with good legs walked through a couple of times without looking at us. Later through an open office door, I saw her sitting on a desk, swinging the legs and talking to someone while she ate cake.

We sat and waited for the doctor. After an hour and a half, the man stood up and said, "Let's get out of here." As we were going to the door, the doctor came in and said, "Well now, what seems to be the trouble?" It was the chesty woman who had been sitting on the desk eating cake.

Sometimes the Cape Cod volunteers were called to go to one of the bridges over the canal that divides Cape Cod from the rest of Massachusetts.

Originally there was a small river that ran part of the way across the neck of the Cape. In 1880, to save the coastal shipping from the long perilous journey around the shoals at the outer end, five hundred Italian workmen with shovels and wheelbarrows began to dig out the river bed into what is now the Cape Cod canal.

There were ferries at first, then drawbridges, and the elegant towered railroad bridge, whose span still rumbles pensively down and up once a day, even when there are no trains. In 1933, the two soaring road bridges, high enough for the tallest ships, were built at Bourne and Sagamore, with a walkway at the side, and a railing only waist high.

The bridges have been favorite places for suicides ever since. Because it's so easy. Because it's almost certain death. The fall from a hundred and thirty five feet into swiftly running and often turbulent water is like hitting a concrete pavement from a skyscraper. People may imagine that it is less violent to jump off a bridge and be swept away by the water's merciful embrace, but they usually die of terrible injuries rather than drowning, or they drown because they are knocked out or badly injured.

The beautiful bridge is not only easy. It is also there. Its presence exerts a sinister fascination. It draws unhappy and disturbed people like a magnet, and the more deaths there have been, the more the legend grows. One person who jumps is likely to be followed by others, if there has been publicity. If you seem to be nobody in life, here's a chance at least to be famous for being dead.

When people talk about what will happen after their suicide—"You'll read it in the papers," "Everyone will be sorry then"—you may have to remind them that they won't be here to enjoy the spotlight. Sometimes it is a simple, practical thing like this that can stem the urgency of a suicidal crisis.

"Who'll feed the dog?"

By 1979, after more than 60 deaths, "going to the bridge" had become Cape Cod's synonym for suicide.

"I can't take it anymore." A call would come to the Samaritans. "If things don't get better, I'll go to the bridge."

"I've been thinking of the bridge all week. I can't get it out of my mind."

"I went to the bridge last night. I walked across and looked at the water. Why am I such a coward?"

Sometimes the voice came from a call box near one of the bridges. "I'm going to jump!"

Why did they ring us? Why hadn't they already jumped?

For the same reason that a man may call to say that he has the telephone in one hand, and a loaded revolver in the other. Because suicide is almost never a simple, determined decision, there is a tug between life and death. People want to jump, and yet don't want to.

When they tell us, "I'm going to jump," they really mean, "I'm terrified I might jump."

If somebody called from the bridge, we said we would come to them, and then tried to keep them talking until a volunteer got there.

Sometimes the police would ask for one of us to go and talk to someone they had found on the bridge. The room at the police station is quite bleak, and in the middle of the night, the coffee is old and gritty. We would usually take the person to the all-night restaurant at the end of the bridge, and talk across a table, often until after dawn. Sharing food with someone brings you closer, and can make talking easier.

Jim went to a man wanted by the police. Steve went to someone who had walked out of a mental hospital and hitchhiked to the bridge. Ann traveled to the house of a woman near the bridge who was going to jump with her little dog in her arms. Jean went out to look for a caller she knew who kept ringing and hanging up from different call boxes. She found him walking slowly across the bridge, and stopped her car and opened the door.

"Fred." With drivers already blowing their horns behind, there was no time for sweet talk. "Get in this car and get away from here."

A young divorced woman, hideously depressed, not coping, had left her child with her mother and gone to the Sagamore bridge to drive over and over, around the circle at each end, back and forth for two hours. When the voice of the bridge finally said to her impassively, *If you're going to do it, do it,* she stopped her car and went for the rail. As she went over, she thought, "My God, what am I doing? I don't want to die. . . ."

She grabbed at steel cables, and because she had gloves on, was able to hang on just long enough for a passing driver to grab her and pull her back.

"What did he say to you?"

"He yelled out, 'You can't do it!'" She told Ruth at the police station. "He was very strong. I thought it was God."

One night, Ellen talked for a long time to a despairing man whose drinking had lost him his wife and children, and now another woman he loved. He would not tell her where he was, but finally he said, "I'm at the bridge."

"I'm coming."

After two hours in the restaurant, Ben said he was all right, and was going to get his car and go home. Following him out, Ellen saw him turn away from the car park and run up onto the bridge. A driver saw him climb over the rail, and by the time she got there, the police were there too, and the bridge traffic had been stopped. Ben was standing on a girder, with his head below the level of the roadway, looking out at the stretch of moonlit water.

Leaning over the rail, saying whatever she could to keep him from jumping—what does one say? Afterwards you can hardly remember—she was too far away. She could only see the back of his head and shoulders, could only hear some of his bitter, hopeless words. Under the bridge, the Coast Guard boat chugged gently against the tide.

There was a six-inch gap under the railing. By lying in the road, Ellen was able to get her arm through and reach down.

"Turn around Ben. Turn around and hold my hand."

Slowly, he turned, and she was able to reach his hand.

"Come back up."

"No." But he clung tightly to her hand.

How long they stayed like that, what it was that made him sigh at last, and say, "I'm coming up," she could not remember afterwards.

"No police."

She turned her head from the rail and with her free hand, told the police and the other people to get back.

"No police, Ben."

He let go of her hand and grabbed at the steel framework, and looked up for the first time, agonized, his face drained white. As he climbed up, a man reached over to help him over the railing, and he collapsed into the road.

Ellen sat limply beside him. A priest had appeared from somewhere, and the three found themselves saying a sort of prayer, sitting with their backs against the railing and their feet stuck out into the road.

Another night when I was on call, a young man had climbed over the railing and crawled along a girder below the bridge, under the middle of the roadway. It was a black night of wind and rain. Various people were trying to shout at him over the railings on either side, but he could not hear us, and we could not hear him. A girl who had been with him when he stopped the car without warning and ran for the rail, said that he had been drinking and had drugs with him.

The Coast Guard boat was below, with a spotlight trained on the man on the girder. Would someone like to go under the bridge in another boat and try to talk to him through a loudspeaker?

Thank God for the instinct that had made me throw an extra sweater and gloves in the car. The police took me to the Coast Guard farther down the canal. As the boat neared the bridge, I could see Jack miles above us in the beam of light, sitting on the girder. He looked like a fly.

I could not see or hear whether he responded to any of the things I shouted at him through the bullhorn. What did I say? Whatever it was, the whole of southeastern Massachusetts could hear it. At one point, Jack threw down what looked like a paper bag. Probably pills. The bag took a long time to reach the water. I'll die if he jumps, I thought.

He jumped. With a yell, he threw himself outwards, sprawling, clutching at the air. After an eternity, he hit the water feet first, and disappeared. The body came up, slumped over, face in the water, held up by the air in the humped jacket.

The other boat was there. They fished him over the side, shouted to us, "He's alive!" and we churned back to the dock.

He was lying in a well at the bow of the other boat. When I knelt beside him, he raised his plastered eyelashes and looked at me, and winked. His skin was ashen, drawn back against the skull, his teeth chattering, his body shaking and rigid under the blankets.

As they came to lift him out, he said, "Did you hear the one about . . ." and told me some feeble, grubby joke.

The ambulance men, doing the necessary things as we drove to the hospital, made feeble jokes too, like, "Thought you'd take an early morning swim, hey fellow?"

Later that day, after they found out that he had no injuries except bruises on his chest and the soles of his feet, he told me that when he was a child, he used to stay with his parents in the campground under the bridge. When he started to get into trouble and could not get his life straight, he began to think that one day he would go back to the bridge and jump. "Something I had to do."

That night, a friend brought some clothes to the hospital, and Jack discharged himself against medical advice.

I did not see him again.

At about this time, we got permission from the Army Corps of Engineers to put up signs at each end of both bridges. Nobody wanted us to use the word suicide—not good for tourism—so the four large signs, which everyone must see coming onto or leaving Cape Cod, now say, "DESPERATE? CALL THE SAMARITANS," with our telephone number.

They brought us many calls, sometimes from people who saw them every day going to and from work, sometimes from people who saw them for the first time when they went to the bridge in despair.

But people were still jumping. Long ago, I had asked whether anyone had thought about putting up a higher railing on the bridges.

"Bad for tourism," came up again, and "If you stop them in one place, they'll do it in another."

A more reasonable objection was the problem of increased weight and wind resistance. In 1978, however, the engineers announced a four year plan to repair and strengthen the two bridges. Now was our chance.

They were having an "environmental impact" meeting in Bourne, so I went along with Barbara to sit in the back row and listen to engineers and environmental analysts talk about traffic flow and falling paint and extra police and salt corrosion.

After a few questions from the handful of people in the hall— "That's it then," the engineers and analysts cheerfully began to put the papers back into their briefcases. "If there are no more questions . . ."

Now or never. I stood up. Barbara pretended not to know me.

"Just one thing."

Why was I suddenly dry-mouthed? I had been speaking in public for years, about suicide and other things. The backs of my legs were trembling, as I had seen the nylon calves of countless program chairmen of women's clubs tremble as they mewed into the microphone that no one had remembered to turn on. "Ay-und now, ladies, it is my great pleasure to innerdoos you to our speaker. We regret that our own Mollie Bixbee and her festive hats could not be with us after all, but here is Miz Monica Digguns—daughter—granddaughter—of that gray-und old man of littitewer. . . ."

"May we have your question, Ma'am?"

"It's about suicide."

The engineers stopped putting papers in their briefcases and made their faces serious. The handful of audience paused in the act of putting on jackets, and turned around to look at me.

"Would you like to come up front?"

It was a small audience and a short speech, but perhaps the most important one I have ever had to make. I told them why it was literally vital to build a higher fence. I told them how many lives had been needlessly lost, and how many distressed and confused people were tempted to jump, almost against their will. I told them what "Going to the bridge" meant, and about the woman who had hung onto one of the cables, and Ben on the girders in the moonlight, and other people we had known at the bridges, who did not really want to die.

"But if you stop them in one place, won't they go and do it in another?"

"People don't switch plans so easily. And being suicidal isn't a constant state. If you can keep people alive when they are desperate enough for suicide, they have a chance to think of something else they might be able to do, besides kill themselves."

I told them about the study done at the Golden Gate bridge, in which they had followed up for twenty years the many people who had tried to jump and been stopped, or who had jumped and lived. Several of them were dead now, but less than five percent of those by suicide.

The men with briefcases listened very politely. I did not expect to hear anything more from them. We were wondering who we should talk to next on a higher level, when the final report came through the mail about the renovation program. In it was described and sketched in loving detail the eight-foot-high curving steel barrier to be erected on both bridges.

In June 1981, the last section of the barrier was locked into place on the Bourne bridge, the first major road bridge in the United States to have a suicide barrier. I got letters from people with bridges all over the country and from England too, asking wistfully how we got the government to spend the time and money.

I don't know. I honestly don't know. We asked, and they did it.

The Sagamore bridge barrier was finished two years later. Since 1983, "Going to the Bridge" has meant nothing more sinister than driving across the Cape Cod canal to the mainland of Massachusetts.

A few status quo people have called to complain, "You've spoiled the view," although actually, as you drive past the railings, the spaces between them merge and the vertical rods disappear.

Once it was a complaint from a caller who keeps the thought of suicide alive to relieve the monotony.

"Why did you put up those barriers? You've stopped me from jumping."

That was the general idea.

After two years in the tiny choirboys' room under the church, we struck it lucky in Falmouth. The town offered us a large space upstairs in the old Academy, which was built in 1834 so that sons and daughters of Falmouth's farmers and whaling captains could learn Greek and Latin and mathematics.

It is a beautiful four-square white wooden building, with Greek Revival pillars at the front and a cupola on top for the old school bell. The bell rope dangles through the roof into a little room where we answer the telephone, a fitting reminder that our business is suicide, and we must always give people the chance to talk about it, if that is what is on their minds.

The cry for help is sometimes masked, because suicide is secret and forbidden. We may need to ask something like, "Is it bad enough to make you think of suicide?" so as not to miss the real, despairing reason for the call.

An answer, "Yes, but I've never told anyone," or "I think about it all the time," can be the beginning of the release of tension, a crack in the dam for the pent-up pain that must be heard, and shared.

Asking someone about suicide doesn't put the idea into their heads. If they are not suicidal, they'll be glad to tell you so. If they are, you need to know.

Asking someone about suicide—a friend, a relation, a colleague, even a stranger, on one of those chance encounters when somebody opens up to you—is something that anyone can do. Must do, if things seem bad enough. You don't need to be an expert to try to help a suicidal person to stay alive. You need to be able to give them a chance to talk about the worst of it, and then to keep quiet and listen.

9

There are Samaritan branches all over the world. It is exciting and encouraging to visit far-off countries and find the same kind of volunteers offering the same kind of befriending to people with the same kind of need, under all different kinds of local conditions.

Some, like Singapore, have to be able to answer the telephone in six or seven different languages. Calcutta spends almost as much time caring for the dying as for the living. The Belfast center is one of the few places in that country where Catholics and Protestants can work amicably together. In Sri Lanka, at Sumithrayo—The Singhalese word for friendship—the bare little concrete hut on a hill above a lake in Kandy, hears as much about sex problems as anything else. Women are emerging into different kinds of wives, and many husbands feel emasculated by the idea of doing sex *with* somebody, rather than *to* somebody.

In Hong Kong, the Chinese branches add extra phone lines at exam time, to take the increased calls from anxious and desperate children. In isolated parts of Scotland, a lot of befriending is done by mail. In countries where there are few telephones and few who could write a letter even if there was a proper mail service, people will walk sometimes two or three days to the place where there is someone to talk to.

In America we now have several branches, and more are being opened every year. From that tentative beginning at the Arlington Street Church, when we fell over each other to welcome the postman or any cheerful drunk who stumbled down our steps, Boston has become the busiest branch in the world.

Three hundred calls and visits a day, and all the other branches almost as busy in proportion to their population. . . . Is this what that high-powered woman at the early board meeting meant by a "felt need"?

Although I had seen how the Samaritans grew in Britain from Chad's tiny beginning in the crypt of St. Stephen's to almost two hundred branches and twenty thousand volunteers, I never expected it to grow like this in the United States. If I had, I might not have floundered into it so blithely with my "Can I tell you about the Samaritans? There's—er—there's these volunteers all over the world, and they befriend suicidal people. . . ."

Avery Wiseman, the psychiatrist who helped me at the very beginning because he liked the idea of "offering service without being burdened by scientific theories and hypothesis," told me years later, "If you had had any more experience of what you were in for, you wouldn't have risked it in the first place—like getting married."

You could probably say the same of each man or woman who gets the urge to start the Samaritans in a new place.

When I hear them say with shining eyes, "I'm going to start a branch," I think, "There goes at least two single-minded years of your life. You don't know what you're in for." But I tell them what Chad told me: "All you need is moral courage," and as time goes on, we talk about other things they will need as well.

We have put together a national organization now, to help new branches to start and old ones to keep going, and to see that the powerful simplicity of Chad Varah's original idea—to make the right kind of ordinary people instantly available to those who need them—does not get corrupted or distorted or diluted.

With so many people involved, it becomes easier to start, even though many of the places are hundreds or thousands of miles away. But however much help you can get from others who've been through it all before, you still have to make your own discoveries and your own mistakes. And each new person who takes on the responsibility is going to have those sleepless nights of doubt and terrible anxiety.

I can't do it. It's too big for me. What do I know anyway?

But there can be no turning back, because there are always the people who come to join you, to lead or push you forward. And although a lot of the things you used to set store by are going to go out of the window, the gains for you will outstrip everything else.

Apart from the reward of being allowed into people's lives at a time when they need you, and of making it possible for a whole continuing crowd of volunteers to know that satisfaction, you have added an absorbing new interest and purpose to your own life.

Look at me. A whole new obsession discovered in middle age. The chance to go on working hard. To make all these droves of new friends. To feel still useful.

A whole new life. I am vigorous and content. I exhaust everyone by myself with my energy.

Suicides are increasing all over the world, and even in Britain, where the figures had dropped dramatically twenty years after the Samaritans had started, the rate is creeping up again.

With the whole world at risk from nuclear suicide, perhaps it is not surprising that individual sojourners get to wondering whether it is worthwhile going on. Yet this is never the main reason given for planning suicide. It's always something more singular and personal, the immediate pain of which makes global affairs irrelevant.

The most disturbing thing about the increase in suicides is that in the Seventies and Eighties, the greatest rise had been among the young. In the United States, it is now the second most common cause of death for people under twenty. The first is car accidents. The third is murder.

An adolescent's suicide attempt is sometimes an impulsive reaction to a loss or rejection or failure; sometimes the consummation of a long love affair with death. Whether it has been brewing for years, or only hours or minutes, the act itself is often impulsive, rather than deliberate, and death, if it results, more accidental than totally intended.

"When I cut my wrist," a young girl said, "when I did actually put the razor blade to the skin, at that precise second, I knew I wanted to die. As soon as the edge sliced through and the skin parted and the blood welled up, I realized I didn't want to be dead."

Another girl spoke up during a talk in her school, and defined quite openly, to me and the whole class, the purposes of wrist-cutting.

"It's not because you want to bleed to death," she said. "There are easier ways to die. But when the tension is so unbearable, it's the only way to get release. It doesn't hurt till you get to the tendons. You cut, and then the pain flows out along with the blood."

Conversation in an emergency room:

> "Why did you take the pills?"
> "I don't know."
> "Did you know they could kill you?"
> "I don't know. Maybe."
> "Did you want to die?"
> "I guess so. No. I don't know. I didn't think about that."
> "Then why did you take them?"
> "They been sitting there looking at me."
> "And telling you to kill yourself?"
> "Nah. Just to take them."

Someone may take two or three pills from a full bottle, wanting to die as they go from hand to mouth, but as soon as they are swallowed, may call someone like the Samaritans to say, in effect, "Help. I'm afraid I may take the rest."

Most adolescent suicide attempts are made at home, using something that belongs at home. The mother's tranquilizers, the father's gun, the kitchen disinfectant, the family car in the enclosed garage.

Why at home? Punishment for the parents? More like hope—even subconscious hope—of rescue.

Poems and diaries bear witness to dreams of death. Teenage magazine advice columns get hundreds of suicidal letters:

"I don't belong anywhere or to anyone, and I would be so much better off if I had never been born. At least when I'm dead, no one will miss me."

"I'm sure I am one of the ugliest people in the world, if not the very ugliest. I'm fat and clumsy. I have few friends other than whose who pity me. After fifteen years, I can no longer stand it."

"Dear God, what the hell is wrong with me? I've completely lost my way and will to study. I feel so hopeless. Christ, I am so depressed. I'm a loner. I hate myself so much. God help me, I don't want to be like this. All I can say is, I've got to die. What the hell is wrong with me?"

But these letters are usually anonymous, without an address. The diaries and poems are often not seen by anyone else until it is too late. Even if they are shown, or left lying about in the hope that someone will pay some attention, they may not be taken seriously.

> Plunge deep in the tidal waters
> .....cold dash of sorrow
> Bitter-sweet breezes
> Sweep the last of your dreams
> away with you.

Oh, teenagers are naturally morbid. It's just a phase.

It is true that the awkward, ambivalent journey towards growing up has always been shadowed by melancholy, and mystical images of death. Victorian girls used to sit on tombstones and write tear-drenched verse. When I was young, we used to go to the top of a hill and dream of casting our sorrow out into the valley, and ourselves with it, never falling, just floating eternally into hopelessness. We hated our lives and our families and most of all ourselves. We traveled through melancholia, but I don't think many of us were close to suicide. Now they are. Now they are killing themselves on the journey.

10

After we had started in Boston, Shirley, Sally and I began going out to give talks wherever we could get an invitation.

In those days, when we were still a slightly bizarre novelty, we got into some surprisingly high class places. I remember confidently addressing medical, psychiatric and nursing staff of several hospitals; medical students, and other big classes, at Radcliffe, Harvard and Tufts, and other splendid universities; Jesuit seminaries, and even the American Psychiatric Association, with not much to offer except a brash enthusiasm and an idea that the audiences seemed to enjoy discussing suicide from a single, practical viewpoint, as a change from theories, case histories and theology.

I was less nervous then than I often am now, before an audience, because of that kindly law which swaddles the innocent tyro: the less you know, the less you know how much you don't know.

Also, it is easier to make statements about suicidal people when you have only talked to a few dozen of them. When you have talked to hundreds, you realize that although they may have elements in common, each individual, each situation is different, and needs their own approach.

In 1974, suicide was generally considered a secret mistake, that should be swept under the rug. It happened, but to other people, and must be in some way their fault.

Don't let on to that girl in the office that you know why she was in the hospital. Don't ask Mrs. Jones about her son who blew his brains out. She won't want to talk about it.

With my usual luck, our second year in the church basement coincided with the waning of a particular interest cycle of five years, which is the upper limit for anything to stay fashionable and newsworthy in this country of shifting fads.

Everyone (except the kids) was getting bored with Drugs in Schools. Drugs was an old story, becoming hard to get newsprint and air time for. What next? Suicide began to be the coming thing, especially adolescent suicide. Drugs were still going on, but the impression was that the problem was less, because there was less talk about it. Suicide, how shocking! Let's cozy up to that with our sincere, concerned faces and our blazers with the television network crest on the pocket.

So it was not hard for us to get publicity, and it has not been difficult since to get many of the schools to let us come in and discuss depression and suicide with students and staff.

Talking in schools is mostly enjoyable, but it has its traumas. Morning classes are better, because more people yawn and nod off and fall on the floor after lunch. But too early in the morning means they are not yet awake, at the daybreak hours when school starts business, to get the kids back on the street by two p.m., long before Mom gets home from work.

Usually the classes are quite vocal, and they like to make jokes and guess which state of the union has the most suicides. (They always guess their own, wherever you happen to be.) But sometimes you hit a class that sits mute as tombstones. You knock yourself out trying to get a response from those closed faces and unfocused eyes. Getting none, you are forced to deliver a monologue to keep the thing going until the shrill buzzer empties the room in ten seconds, and then there are complaints afterwards that it was a lecture, not a discussion.

I shall never forget a dreadful afternoon at a high school in rural Massachusetts. I was to speak in the library to a "select group" of seniors, guaranteed to be attentive and interested.

There were comfortable chairs in one corner, and three or four of the young men made for them. A pair of girls went to the book shelves and began to read standing up. The others sat down at different tables, most of them with their backs to me.

A cool-looking customer in a pink angora sweater sat at a table right in front of me. Good. Here was one of the attentive ones. She opened a folder to make notes. I started to speak. She started to write a letter, with the paper turned sideways so that her cramped hand was writing from bottom to top.

I managed to get the other students somewhat involved by asking around the group a question that was easy to answer in different ways. When I came to pink angora, she did not answer, or look up, or stop writing. Panic rose in me. What do teachers *do*?

I made mistake number one. I said, "I'm sorry, but you have to answer."

She flicked me a brief defiant glance, and went on with her letter.

Mistake number two. My panic heated up into anger. "One of us," I heard myself says, "is going to have to leave this room."

She did look up then, with bold blue eyes that said as clearly as her scornful mouth would, if it had ever opened, "Go ahead."

Mistake number three. I totally lost my temper. Red and fuming, I looked around the select group. The armchair ones were playing cards on an atlas held on someone's knee. A boy at one of the tables had his hand up a girl's sweater. Some of the backs turned to fronts to watch what I would do. Two teachers behind me were shrinking into the book stacks, wishing I had not made mistake number one.

Seeing my face, one of them got up and took the girl gently out of the room.

"She has a problem," they told me afterwards. So did I. I knew that she had won.

An alternative high school can be more fun than a regular one. This is a separate school within a school for people who don't seem to benefit from conventional education. They may be no great shakes at learning, but they are often quite sophisticated and dashing, and very relaxed and genial in their attitude toward whoever is trying to teach them something.

Feet wearing enormous boots with soles like tractor treads (male and female) are comfortable lodged on the desks, and they watch you tolerantly through them, as if you were a television screen in a motel. Other feet are bare, or in colorful odd socks, and their owners lie on the floor and observe you from below. Their teacher, if there is one— sometimes you are left alone with this misfit group because they are safe—looks like something left over from the Sixties, his gentle voice venturing hesitantly out of the straggly beard, in which he caresses a single hair while you talk.

All these young ones are interested in talking about crisis and despair. Many of them have been through it. Interestingly, they are often better able to discuss how you hang onto life and make it work than their more conventional contemporaries.

A few weeks ago, I answered the telephone to a college professor who was having a bad night and needed someone to ease her off the three a.m. treadmill of circular thinking.

I didn't need to say much. It did her good to talk, but as she said goodbye before turning off her light to try to sleep, she said, "I never thought I'd call you people." And went on to tell me that two or three years ago, she had invited a Samaritan speaker to one of her psychology classes. "And I wished I hadn't. I wasn't impressed at all." The name? She had forgotten. A merciful oblivion.

Oh dear. What volunteer had I sent out not properly prepared or trained? I padded through the dark center outside the telephone room and groped for the light switch to look for the old calendars.

It was me who had gone to speak to that psychology class. I remembered them now. I thought it had gone rather well. Oh Lord, let it be good for me to be thus humbled, to make the hurt of it worthwhile.

Good thing she had not needed me to say much tonight. She obviously had not recognized my voice, even with its mongrel transatlantic accent which sometimes provokes the inquiry, "What's the matter—are you Australian? or the drunken command, "Brits, get out of Northern Ireland."

At another university where I was the nervous one of a panel of what they lyrically call suicidologists, a psychologist who was lulling the audience with statistics, mentioned that two doctors in this city had killed themselves in the last six months.

Up out of the audience like an electric spark jumped a small middle-aged woman and shouted, "And one of them was my husband!" German or Austrian, intense with emotion.

"You killed him!" she cried out. "He tried to talk to people here who he thought were his friends. They told him to take some time off. He went for therapy to a colleague—I don't say who, you all know who—and was given pills. Nobody would listen. Nobody paid attention. He died—" she swept around with her arm flung out to appeal to the stricken audience—"he died for lack of love."

Someone took her arm and tried to lead her out, but she brushed off their hand and sat down again quite composed, folded her arms and poised her head to hear what came next.

She gave me some courage. It helps if you can find at least one special face in the audience which seems to be sending you messages. When it was my turn to speak, I spoke to her.

During these years when suicide has been hot news, indeed somewhat overdone, because soon no one will want to hear any more (adolescent alcoholism is the new diversion), television and radio have given us a lot of publicity.

When you are on a radio talk show where listeners call in, you find that you already know some of the lonely people who regularly call the station, because they are also regularly calling the Samaritans. The talk show host bustles them off the air as quickly as possible, because they don't make good radio.

Nor is good radio made by the adorable people who call in to the show to say that our volunteers have helped them. They get bustled off, too, because the host suspects that I have planted them.

The people who do make good radio, alas, are the desperate and suicidal ones who will lay bare their agony and despair to thousands of listeners driving cars or folding laundry or ironing or carpentering or on a factory bench, with the radio half heard as background music.

As a radio guest, it's difficult. If you had this unhappy person on the telephone, you wouldn't say much, and would hope that they would stay talking to you for a long time. But on the air, you've got to be more articulate, and you've got somehow to capsule the conversation, because if the news or a commercial comes up, the caller may get cut off.

Why do people choose a radio show to make the cry for help? How can she *say* all that, in her tin-can voice which must be recognizable, about her drinking and her failed marriage? Why does this man want to tell the world about his self disgust?

Fleeting notoriety. Pain needs to shock. Forlornness needs attention. Perhaps despair seeks drama.

There was a woman in New York who thought that she was condemned to die from cancer. She decided to commit what she called rational suicide, a sort of self-euthanasia, deliberately planned and logically desired. Fair enough. It does happen, either with or without the knowledge or help of a merciful doctor. What made this woman's death different was that she chose to play it out in front of a vast audience.

Jo, who had always felt that her parents only accepted her as a replacement for a beloved older sister who had died, had been trying to kill herself in symbolic as well as real ways ever since she grew up. She changed her first name three times. She gave away the small children of her first marriage when her young husband died. She was heavily into drugs, and made several suicide attempts, including a failed suicide pact with a lover who chickened out, and helped her to sleep it off.

She married twice more, the last time happily. She had become a successful artist and a psychotherapist. She had another daughter and a lot of friends . . . and she decided that now was the time to set the final date for her suicide.

The news of the cancer was not the cause, but the confirmation of this long-range plan, and advanced the date of it by several years. By this time, she had persuaded a lot of her New York friends that rational suicide was the way to go. Some of them were even involved in her plans for an Exit House, where people could kill themselves in comfort, or have it done for them.

One of her friends was a film maker. He agreed to videotape some interviews with her, and to film Jo's last party. After she died, the film and tapes were shown on nationwide television.

It is rather a dull film. Queen Jo moves among her admiring husband, daughter and friends, poor darling, middle-aged now and hefty in a broad pink caftan, and all these clever, enlightened New York people who accept her imminent death speak words of love, and indulge in what looks like a rather sycophantic necrophilia.

"Dying is easy," she says. "This is something for me . . . for all of us. I want to die on a day when I feel well and in command of myself, and when I can know that I am making my choice. It is my life's canvas, and I'm going to end it my way."

The most believable people at the party are two rather square relations from the Middle West, wrongly dressed for the arty gathering, the woman's hair teased up and lacquered. But when this couple speak, suddenly it's the others who don't fit.

"Don't do it, Jo," they say. "It's wrong. We don't want you to do it."

At the end of the hour's film, anyone still watching can see Jo drink champagne with her husband and daughter, and go into her own room to take the fatal dose of seconal. The only thing missing is a rifle shot, just before the credits roll.

After her death, her husband and daughter appeared on another television program. They repeated the things that Jo had said: "Suicide is a liberator, enricher, clarifier of life." They talked about quality of life and the need to be in control. The daughter said that she would let her children watch their grandmother go to her death on film.

"Better for them than watching her die of cancer."

Self-termination is self-determination, they said. They were quiet and even-voiced and unemotional. They both looked rather thin and tired. Jo's husband seemed a lot less confident than he had been in the film made before she died. After all, she was still alive then, however brave the talk of death. There was still the chance that she might change her mind.

One of the things that Jo had told her family and friends at that last party was, "You'll like me better."

Her widower is a psychologist. Does he ever wonder if that was not the woman speaking, but the child, who always thought her mother loved her elder, dead daughter more?

My dear Sarah, who killed herself in the hospital, also appeared on television, to talk about life.

About a year before she died, a Boston station was making a short documentary about the Samaritans, and Sarah wanted to be in it.

We couldn't discourage her. On a cold, sunny day, the cameraman walked backwards along a path on Boston Common, while Sarah, very small, walked by the side of tall willowy Rebecca 92, who had wept crocodile tears with me at the gimmicky psychotherapist's. Sarah turned up her sweet bright face, and Rebecca bent down her calm gentle face, and Sarah talked about her many suicide attempts, and how she had avoided other ones, and how glad she was to find herself alive.

She was marvelous. She made the program. "I'm a star!" she said. She was happy that day.

Several times a year, a group of us spend the morning at one of the police academies. The class is a mixture of new recruits and men and women who have been out on the street for some time.

To some of them, suicide has meant talking people down off high places, cutting someone down from a hanging (usually too late), finding a way to get into a house where a man with a gun is threatening to shoot himself, and perhaps someone else first.

We talk in small groups around tables about the things they see, the strain they are under, the difficulties of a police marriage (your wife either wants to know all the gory details, or never wants to hear anything), and of social life (people either corner you at parties to ask a favor, or shun you as if you were a spy).

They talk about suicides they have been called out to, and hangings in police lockups—usually a young man after his first arrest—and the women complain about the cynicism and tough talk with which some of the men defend themselves against the danger of sympathy.

They talk about the high number of police suicides, mostly with the officer's own gun, and what it is like to be indiscriminately hated.

Last time, one of the Samaritans asked, "What about all the people like me who are glad to see a police uniform, because it looks like help?"

"Yeah, but." One of the older men shook his head sadly. "We don't hardly ever get to meet those people. Most of the time—let's face it—we're dealing with the shit of this world."

11

One day in Boston, one of the local sheriffs called us to his office to discuss a brilliant idea.

He knew that we were short of volunteers at the moment, and very busy. He was not short of men in his jail, and they were not busy at all. We had too much to do. They had nothing to do. We were a twenty-four-hour service. The jail never closed either.

Presto. Hook up one of our telephone lines to the jail and let the men take some of the calls.

Telephones had just been installed, and he wanted them used. As it turned out, the men could not leave their cells at night, and the phones were in the officers' day room, where there was no privacy. So luckily we did not have to dampen his enthusiasm or insult his institution, of which he was very proud. He was the one who said it would not work.

But impossible ideas can sometimes be pulled earthwards and developed into something that is possible and good. There had recently been a suicide in this prison. A young man with the beautiful name of Apollo had been arrested for the third time in a year for mugging someone at knife point for money to support his heroin addiction. On admission, he could name no next of kin, no friends. His parents had been killed in a car accident when he was a child, and he did not know his sister's married name.

During the long wait for trial in the jail, he got no letters and no visitors. He kept saying that people were coming—his girlfriend, his buddy, his sister—but no one ever came.

With his record, he thought he would go to the state prison at Walpole, a penitentiary much feared. When the sheriff spoke to him before his trial, Apollo wept and said, "I'll never survive at Walpole."

Next day, he hung himself by his bootstrings from the heating grill in his cell. With difficulty. The grill was too low, and he had to hold his feet up.

The body waited at the funeral parlor, and when nobody could be traced who knew Apollo, the inmates asked if they could hold the funeral at the jail.

It was the first of its kind, and very moving. Officers and inmates chipped in for flowers. Mass was said in the gym and everyone was there, except those in solitary confinement or protective custody. They had pallbearers and a choir, and Apollo was taken with the flowers to the cemetery and buried in a potter's grave.

This was the sheriff's first suicide. It was the lonely tragedy of Apollo that had prompted his call to us, and the idea that inmates might somehow be able to help others.

All right then, but why not each other? Why not put the Samaritan concept of befriending into the jail and have inmates helping inmates?

When high-flying ideas suddenly come to earth as possible projects, you grab them immediately. Balked of his original idea about the telephones, wanting to do something, the sheriff went into action with us right away. He told the chaplain to run the program, although he did not tell him what or how, because nobody knew, and we had our first meeting at the jail.

Bob, the chaplain, had talked to some of the men. Sure, they said, we'll try anything. A natural response from bored, confined men to anything new, especially one that would give them contact with outsiders.

We held the first meeting in the sheriff's office, outside the inner barred gate that leads into the prison. There were three or four Samaritans, someone from the Human Services department, the jail nurse, one or two of the more broadminded officers, and several inmates.

A man called Victor, who had been in prison a long time and was a big wheel here, was naturally one of the men who volunteered. If something was going to start, Victor was going to mastermind it. The sheriff was not with us, nor the jail master or his deputies, so Victor sat in the sheriff's padded swivel chair and put his feet on the sheriff's polished desk and dominated the conversation, dropping names to impress us.

"My attorney . . . my wife's psychiatrist, Dr. Gulag. You must know him. . . ."

Afterwards when the men had gone back through the heavy, barred gate, and we were driving the twenty miles back to Boston, we felt depressed. One of the officers had been dubious, the other cynical. We had all been a bit intimidated by Victor. He was obviously in it for what he could get out of it. He would ruin the program. How could we get rid of him?

We had made no detailed plans yet. This was a new program in a place new and mysterious to all of us. We had to make it up as we went along. Our next meeting was to start training the jail volunteers. We were taken through the heavy gate, and it slid back in a well-oiled way and locked behind us. There was coffee in the bare room where

Samaritans and prisoners sat on metal chairs and watched each other shyly, and tin lids for ashtrays, and the air was thick with years of cigarette smoke that had blackened the ceiling and the top two feet of the walls.

Victor was not there. The chaplain had magically eliminated him.

"No sweat," Bob told me afterwards. "When you've been in a prison four years, like I have, it's easy to say no—'That's it, see you later'—without it being rough."

We did more training with that first group than we do now many years later, in the other jails where this suicide prevention program has started. These men easily grasp the concept of befriending. They know about depression and despair. They need to learn how to recognize the signs that a man may be suicidal, how great the danger is, and what to do in an emergency.

At that first meeting, we probably tried too hard and gave too much information and expected too much of them. All of them, like those who have come since, were natural befrienders, each in his own style.

Some are content to sit patiently and listen for two, six, ten hours. Some know when to challenge a man at the exact moment when he starts talking rubbish. There is one huge fellow who threatens to beat up people if they are faking suicide attempts for attention, and another who tells them, "If you cut up one more time, I'll kill you." There are reasons why they take him seriously.

At that second meeting, the men were even more anxious than we were. They thought of all the reasons why the program would not work. The officers thought of all the things that would go wrong. The men did not think they could do it. They had absolutely no confidence. They had never been asked to pull anything out of themselves to help someone else. Even some of the Samaritans felt it would not work.

So at the next meeting, we stopped trying to bolster them up, and paid attention to all the anxiety and doubts and fears. We talked about the things that bring people to the brink of suicide, and recognized the possibility in ourselves. When we talked about losses, it turned out that every inmate and officer there, and two of the Samaritans, had been boys whose fathers had died or left them.

They chose a name for themselves: Lifeline. The program started. Five Samaritans—Sally, Steve, Nancy, Jim, and Jenny went out every week in Jenny's Volkswagen to meet with the chaplain and the men. It was killingly hot. The evening traffic got worse and worse. Steve and Nancy got to know each other so well in the back of the cramped car that they had moved into an apartment together before the end of the summer.

After Victor was told, "See you later," he threatened to ruin Lifeline. "As only I can, Rev." But after a few incendiary defamations against Bob, the snitches who had been chosen, the dumb Samaritans, he got bored with our small-time plans and went off to try to ruin another of the sheriff's progressive ideas.

The sheriff had started a lot of new programs in the jail. Education. Alcohol and drug treatment. Fitness. Work release before discharge. Conjugal visits, the second prison in the country to have them—and in a room with a bed. Mississippi, the pioneer jail, gave everybody an hour on Sundays in a chicken coop.

The aggravation of all these new soft-hearted programs was one of the reasons why Bob got so much opposition from the prison staff. One or two were genuinely glad of anything that might improve their relations with the men in their charge, but the general attitude among corrections officers was: This wouldn't be such a bad job if it weren't for the inmates.

A do-gooding sheriff, and now this half-assed notion to keep men from doing other people the favor of killing themselves—"Forget it Rev."

Kind, humorous Bob was down to earth and well liked, but this program stank. Why make something complicated out of something so simple? Suicide? If a man threatened it, you told him, "I'll get the rope." Bring him to his senses. If it doesn't—well, one less of them for my taxes to pay for (as long as he doesn't do it on my tier, on my shift).

A few officers were grudgingly sympathetic to Lifeline because of that fear. If a man under their guard "hangs it up" in his cell, it's a black mark for them, let alone having to cut him down and deal with the effects of a corpse on their tier, which could trigger a riot.

The Human Service people went along with it, because they were told to, but they always thought it was a farce run by amateurs, and said so. The jailmaster, the king pin of the institution, but still under the sheriff, told Bob that he would have to sell the idea of Lifeline to the officers on all the shifts.

Bob had never had a problem selling something—"If you can sell religion, you can sell anything"—but the people responsible for security gave him trouble from start to finish. They were afraid that the Lifeliners would have too much power and freedom. The program was too eggheaded. "If college guys thought this up, college guys ought to be here to work it. We don't do this kind of stuff. We're just here in custody."

The Samaritans were a worse bunch of soft-headed do-gooders than the sheriff.

"Whenever I see a woman coming into a prison," a security man mused, "I ask myself, does she really want to get laid by one of these guys?"

Sally and Jenny and Nancy who came in the Volkswagen were all young and good-looking.

"All these girls want to do is come up here and go jiggle, jiggle, and that's all these men want to see."

But the suicide prevention program started. There are two sections of a county jail: the Jail and the House of Correction. The Jail is where you go when you are waiting for trial, for anything from two weeks to two years. The House of Correction is where you go after sentencing, unless you go for a longer term to a state prison, or unless there is some reason, like the nature of your crime, or your informing, why you wouldn't survive in a state prison.

Our original Lifeliners were in the House of Correction, but because new admissions, especially young first-timers are the greatest suicide risk, we trained some inmates in the Jail as well, and the joint Lifeline meetings were the only place where unsentenced and sentenced men mixed. Another grievance for security.

The Lifeline volunteers tried to meet each new inmate, to see how he'd settle down, and to let him know there was help if he needed it. They learned to watch men who never got any mail, or who got the wrong kind, like a "Dear John" letter. They were allowed to talk to men in the hole, a solitary place where many suicide attempts are made, by any means available, from eating a light bulb to rubbing dirt into a cut finger, to try for blood poisoning.

They paid attention to severely depressed and withdrawn people, and to those in great anxiety just before trial, and great hopelessness after, facing ten years to life.

The officers continued to bad-mouth the program, but we learned from Bob and the men not to worry about that, although we always felt insecure, in the uncharted archipelagos of jail politics, that the program might be cut off, because it was working so well.

"Someone's always bad-mouthing something around here," Bob said. "It's almost a mark of respect."

This "mark of respect" especially began to be seen when the men involved took the program seriously. They were not just in it for what they could get. There were no free cigarettes or extra furloughs. There was spending all night talking to a man in his cell, and being woken at two or three in the morning to go to a youngster who had pulled the sheet off his bed and made a feeble attempt to hang himself.

The only bonus was that this would look good on an application for early parole, or work release.

For us, the most exciting thing was to see what Lifeline did for the Lifeliners. At the weekly meetings, which became increasingly relaxed and friendly, it was fascinating to hear about the people they had talked to, and even more fascinating to see the egos flourish.

For the first time in the lives of most of them—Rocky in and out of jail all his adult life; Franco and Rodge whose upbringing, if you could say that anyone had brought them up, had taught them that they didn't count and never would; Bruce, a genius so burned out from drugs and alcohol that only half his brain cells functioned, but those brilliantly—for the first time in their lives, they were of value because of themselves.

They talked and talked. They were articulate, and loved to tell jokes and terrible jail stories. Often at the meetings the Samaritans said little, and we wondered whether the program could run without us.

"No way," Franco said. "With just the jail running it . . ."—he poked a thumb toward the floor and pulled a face of scorn. "It would get corrupted. We'd corrupt it. Meetings would turn into gripe sessions—the food, the cells, the administration—you guys don't want to hear all that. You want to hear who we talked to, and tell us we done good. You're the only outsiders who come in this place who don't have something to sell—literacy or sobriety—all that shit. Excuse me—all that crap. And you keep on coming. Most do-gooders fade."

Sometimes a new Samaritan would come to a few meetings and say nothing, but listen and watch the men and try not to speculate on why they were locked up in here. If they were shy or nervous, they might stop coming, because they felt so useless.

But at the next meeting, the men would ask, "Where's Betty?" or "What happened to Joe? I liked that guy."

The highlight of that year at the jail was when Bob somehow managed to get a day's furlough for three of his Lifeliners to put on a demonstration at a national conference on suicide in one of the Boston hotels. To quiet security, the sheriff granted the furloughs himself, so that if the men never came back, it would be his fault.

Bob and an officer took them out in handcuffs, in case anyone was watching, and took them off in the car. They all had lunch on Bob in the hotel restaurant, and then out to a superb show that was the most popular session of the whole conference.

They played out three scenes:

A man with a Dear John letter from his girlfriend, telling him not to worry about her, because she was being cared for by his friend.

The news of a grandfather's death—sometimes more poignant than a father's, and not only to men in jail.

A youth whose juvenile years of car stealing and break-ins had caught up with him and put him behind bars for the first time, terrified, angry, abandoned and wanting only to die.

There were no scripts for the scenes. They were half planned, half extempore. The men were natural ham actors, verbal, mature, intuitive. Bob played the man in trouble each time, and the ham actor that was also in him got stimulated by the audience to flights they had not rehearsed, but the Lifeliners followed.

In the scene with the young car thief, a loose-jointed black man with a big pink Afro comb stuck into his hair played the Lifeliner, easy going, casually reassuring. We saw the new prisoner gradually relax and drop his defenses and start to talk.

At the end, one of the moguls in the audience, a big-name expert on jail suicide, rose confidently to his feet, commended the Lifeliner mildly, and delivered a short, incisive lecture on what he should have said, and how he had missed his chance to give the new prisoner advice and answers, and steer the course of his life in new directions.

The young black man stared at him blankly. Then he put a hand on his low-slung hip bone and the other into his hair and said, "Well, Jesus, man, I was only trying to make friends with the guy."

The audience went wild. The "expert" went to the bar.

Lifeline had been in the jail a year, and there had been no suicides. There had been several attempts, perhaps as many as usual—inefficient hangings, small cuttings, aspirin overdoses—which the Lifeliners had intercepted. But the jail had recently had a fire and a few escapes and other disturbances, and the administration was jittery, and wanted to tighten up everything.

The sheriff called me one day out of the blue.

"I'm stopping Lifeline."

"You can't," I said, because it was our program, but forgetting that it was his jail.

"I'm stopping it."

"Why?" I nodded to Sally to listen on another telephone. She was devoted to Lifeline. She looked as if she had been kicked in the stomach.

"We've had two suicides in the last three days."

"What?"

"Didn't you know?"

I didn't, but I wasn't going to say so. I said, "That's no reason to stop a suicide prevention program. It's a reason to work harder at it."

"All this talk of suicide," the sheriff was saying, "puts the idea into people's heads. I know these men. They're suggestible. You start an exercise program for bad backs—and fifty people will immediately have bad backs. They'll jump on any band wagon."

"But if there's nothing to gain . . ."

"Lifeline causes suicide. It puts the idea of suicide into people's minds."

"Who says so?"

"I do, and so does Human Services. And security has never liked it, you know."

He'd been got at. Damn!

One of those suicides was a middle-aged man going back to a state prison for a second dose of big time. The other was new and young and scared.

If you believe that most suicides are attempts that went wrong, unanswered cries for help, these two hangings could be called accidents. They both happened late at night when the Lifeliners were not around, and surveillance of the tier was slack.

We wrote letters to the sheriff to tell him that the deaths were not because of, but in spite of, Lifeline. To explain that if a suicide program does reveal more suicidal people, it's because they are there anyway—to remind him that the bad-back syndrome had long been recognized. Inmates who thought they could get what they wanted by threatening to hang it up were getting a visit from an un-gullible Lifeliner, but nothing extra.

We did not point out that if talking about suicide and inviting people to ask for help was driving them to suicide, that would negate not only the work of Lifeline, but the work of the Samaritans as well.

We tore up all the letters anyway.

Poor old Bob. They tried to buy him off by offering him an emasculated version of his program that might do a little light befriending under the supervision of Human Services, without being called Lifeline—nothing that would suggest suicide—but he turned it down, and so did we.

He gave up the chaplain's post soon after that and took up parish work again in a big impoverished church in a depressed town whence industry had fled.

He got to know the people at the local jail, which made the grim place he had left look like the Ritz.

"How about suicide here?"

"Never had one."

"You carrying them out then, and they're DOA at the hospital?"

"No suicides. We take care of our boys."

"Enough to start a volunteer suicide prevention program run by inmates?"

"Can't have volunteers in jails. Unworkable."

Like the jail, Bob thought.

12

When that first program ended, we were already starting a second one at the notorious Charles Street Jail in Boston, the oldest occupied prison in the country, and since then, other Samaritan branches have started their own Lifelines in local jails.

Suicide is about sixteen times more likely to happen behind bars as outside: often within the first few days, or even the first twenty-four hours.

Most vulnerable is the first offender, usually young, terrified, confused, in a nightmare of anxiety over what will happen to the people at home, as well as to himself. His charge is probably not a violent crime, and drugs and alcohol are likely to be mixed up in it.

Before trial and after sentencing are dangerous times. So, ironically, is just before release when the man is preparing to "wrap up" faces the prospect of that other world where he may have lost everything.

The ways of killing yourself in jail are as many and varied as the reasons for doing it. Hanging is the first choice, with a belt or shoelaces or a sock or shirt, or a bedsheet. If the sheet is wet or twisted, there is less chance of rescue, because it is harder to loosen.

People have drunk bleach, swallowed razor blades, put their heads in plastic bags and their fingers into light sockets. They have overdosed on pints of water, stuffed socks down their throats, or banged their skulls against the floor. One man tied his head to the drain stopper of a sink and filled it with water.

In one Massachusetts jail, a man swallowed the contents of the toilet bowl.

Charles Street Jail is a gray stone Victorian fortress huddled defensively between great white modern hospital buildings. Five thousand new inmates come in each year to wait for trial for anything from two weeks to two and a half years.

The sheriff in charge of this jail wanted us to start a suicide prevention program. The superintendent did not like the idea, so he gave it to the chaplain, with whom he was having a vendetta. See how you like *that*, Reverend.

Reverend David got his own back by liking it. Lifeline became the most important thing in his life, both at Charles Street and in other jails where he has helped to start it.

In the years since our first program got the hatchet, dozens of men worked for Lifeline at other jails, and some of them, trapped in the life that keeps them inside as often as outside, have turned up in that first prison, and started a sort of freelance underground Lifeline again. But without the Samaritans going jiggle, jiggle.

Everywhere Lifeline is started, the same trusty old objections crop up.

It's a threat to security. It will lead to escapes. Well, a Lifeliner and a man he was befriending did once cut through the cell bars and take off; but not for long. The man's girlfriend turned them both in.

At Charles Street, they have made a rule that anyone planning to escape must resign from the program at least a month ahead, so as not to give Lifeline a bad name.

There is always the suspicion that Lifeline contacts and meetings are opportunities for passing drugs, which get passed pretty freely anyway in most of the jails, often brought in by a visiting wife or girlfriend in a little balloon, which she transfers during a kiss. If the man is shaken down by an officer, he swallows the balloon and then throws it up, or waits to excrete it.

In one jail, where there was no chaplain or suitable officer to direct Lifeline, Vernon, one of the local Samaritans, ran it from the outside.

When he first ventured inside, scared, not of the inmates, but of his own inadequacy, Vernon found that he had to contend, not only with hostile staff, but with the Lord of the Jail, a long-time inhabitant, the established leader of this society which has its own structure and laws and internal politics. Sid was president. He had his stooges. He had his extra comforts, including a green plastic toilet seat, greatest of all treasures in a jail where men live three to a cell in the company of a stinking wooden bucket.

New inmates who thought that the administration ran the jail quickly learned at their first meal, "That's Sid. He's in charge here."

Vernon learned, too. He co-opted Sid into Lifeline, where he proved to be a surprisingly good befriender—and defender of the program. The other inmates, who had suspected Lifeline of being a nest of informers and undercover screws, now accepted Vernon and his do-good program, and lay in wait to chat with him as he wandered amicably around the House of Correction.

The officers, however, continued to lock him in on a tier and go away, and not come back with the keys when Vernon wanted to leave. He had to stand forever behind the bars and add his shouts of "Gate!" to the general shouts and bangings that are part of background prison music.

"Why bother?" the men would ask him. "Why not just stay here, Vern?"

One of the perennial objections to Lifeline was that crafty inmates will threaten suicide to get what they want. Of course they will, and so would I. They threaten to kill themselves if they don't get parole, an extra visit, tranquilizers from the doctor, cigarettes, a radio, a cell on the "executive tier." They swallow a few pills or cut themselves to get transferred to "the Ranch," the state psychiatric hospital out in the country, which is no picnic, but freer than jail and easier to escape from.

The Ranch, the Farm (a state prison), the Hill (Block Ten at a worse state prison)—pastoral names that mock brutal reality. The federal penitentiary is the Country Club.

But Lifeline learned how to distinguish between the seriously suicidal person and the games player. Idle threats were taken at their face value. David and the Charles Street Lifeliners took a hard line. The man would be sent down to the suicide cell, a "strip cell," where there was no bed or plumbing, and all his clothes were taken away.

"Hey, listen, fellas. I was just kidding."

"Well, we ain't. You said you're gonna hang it up. O.K. We heard you."

One of the surprises about going into the jails was the sensitive consideration and genuine compassion shown by these men, in an environment that could not be anything but brutal and cynical.

Lifeliners are men of varied backgrounds and education and race and criminal histories. The Samaritans who sit around the table with them every week as colleagues don't know why the men are here, and usually don't speculate.

A new volunteer, wide-eyed after her first meeting, said afterwards, "They're so nice, they can't have done anything that bad. What are they in for—breaking and entering?"

One was a child molester. One shot a policeman. One was a prominent embezzler. One killed his wife.

When Lifeliners are being released, or moved to another jail, replacements are chosen by the men themselves, subject to official approval, which is usually given, unless it's a troublemaker, or someone the jailmaster uses as an informer.

Informers are colloquially known as "dime-droppers," because secret information is usually conveyed by telephone, and you drop in a dime to make a call. (Today, of course, it would be a "quarter-dropper.") If an inmate is suspected of being an informer, someone passing his cell will put a dime outside on the bars as a sign. If he is found out, in the jungle of a state prison like Walpole, he will probably be killed.

"I hear a guy was killed at Walpole for two packs of cigarettes. You can't wonder poor old Eddie doesn't want to go there."

It's a Lifeline meeting at one of the smaller county jails. Eddie, recently sentenced, had cut his wrists mildly—sideways chicken scratches, not a cut into the length of vein that means business—and Vince is reporting.

Vince and Tony talked with him for two hours yesterday. His girlfriend is through with him because of the long sentence, but they report that they think he's stable. The nurse has been helpful. Eddie is on tranquilizers today. He has been checked out before supper by Joe, a burly, silent man with delicate hands and a full handlebar moustache that hides his mouth but lifts at the corners when he smiles.

"He's O.K."

It is like a conversation between colleagues anywhere, relaxed, serious, with room for easy jokes between the three inmates, two Samaritans and Jack, the young officer who runs the meeting, and lets the men do most of the talking. We sit at the big round table in the prison library, where the hardcover books are mostly old and unused, except the law books, and the piles of paperbacks are battered.

After coming through the steel trap between two gates, Ken, a new, young Samaritan, and I have gone through the guardroom, past the observation unit, where a television set flickers and blares canned laughter outside the three cells—if they yell for an officer to change the channel, would anyone come?—down angled iron staircases, along a corridor wide enough for one person, through another gate which is locked behind us, and into the library. The door of the room is locked behind us, and into the library. The door of this room is not locked. There is excellent coffee with a lot of fresh milk, because this jail keeps cows. The ashtrays are wide institution-size soup cans, with one side of the rim bent inwards to rest a cigarette on.

Jack is in uniform. Although it is winter, the men are in green T-shirts, two of them with that extra bulge of the left bicep that is the cigarette pack twisted into the short sleeve, since prison clothes have no pockets. All the jails are much too warm (the prison system could save a bit there). The Samaritans are the only ones wearing sweaters.

Joe, the big man with the moustache, and Tony are in their twenties. Tony is dark-skinned, small and quick, with a grin full of teeth that won't be so white if he goes on chain-smoking. Vince is a bit older than the others, educated, articulate. He was a paper hanger, he has told us, which means bad checks, not wallpaper. All the men have clean and rather stylish hair. There are always people here who can cut hair, and it's the fashion for most inmates to be well barbered.

Joe and Tony have spent time last week with an angry man whose wife had called him for permission to spend the night with her boyfriend.

"Nice of her."

"Bitch," Vince says, but Joe, who has a vast tolerance, says, "She feels bad, so she wants to make damn sure he feels bad too."

Jack goes through the list of last week's customers. Tony, who speaks Spanish, has talked to two of the many men who go through the court and prison system unable to speak English. He was in the shower room at the weekend, checking out the admissions, telling first timers about the jail.

"One kid was crying. It's his first arrest. Manslaughter. He'd heard so many fearsome things about jail, he was surprised when I talked to him. Jeez, I was so nice to the kid, he thought I must be somebody from the outside."

A seventeen-year-old also came in on Saturday on a small, stupid charge. Vince shakes his head. "These kids. Amateurs. Ruin the good name of crime."

"And a couple of nuts," Tony reports. "Weekenders."

For various reasons, including money, mental institutions have been releasing chronic patients without enough continuing support. They get picked up for breaking the law in minor ways they don't understand, and the police bring them to the jail until the mental health system gets geared up on Monday. Sometimes they stay here.

The jail is overcrowded, like all the others. There are not enough of the small domestic jobs, few educational programs, with few participants, nothing for the men to do. A few who have earned the privilege work outside, on the farm. "But most of these young guys," Joe says, "were outside only three or four days all last summer, is all. The screws—sorry," to Jack, "—the officers can't be bothered. It's easier to keep them locked up, watching TV all day. No wonder they beat up on each other, or hurt themselves."

This complaint leads to others more esoteric, and too familiar.

"Gripe number 831," Jack says. "We've heard it before."

"And you will again, man."

The men laugh. But Ken, with untarnished ideals and hopes, who is here for the first time, is troubled by the complaints. He has been troubled since he came through the steel trap, and looked at the men in the barred cages.

"They do *that*?"

Joe has been feeding horrors to Ken's open, sympathetic face.

"But that's inhuman. That's not fair."

This actually has a better effect than "Gripe Number 831." Joe, who was only griping to keep in practice, tells him, "Look, the whole system's unfair. But you got to remember this, Ken. No one put us in here. We put ourselves in here."

Jack has news from the Ranch about George, who tried to hang himself two weeks ago and was sent away for observation. The Lifeliners had spotted George as a suicide risk, and had tried to help him. They were shaken by the hanging. The man was just cut down in time, and resuscitated. They share with the Samaritans the self-doubts and the frustration of having tried to help someone, and failed.

"Makes you mad too," Tony admits. "If I saw that guy, I'd say, 'All that time I spent with you, and you go and do a dumb thing like that.'"

But the serious suicide attempt has made a stir in the jail. Things had been quiet for some time, and this has reminded the Lifeliners that suicide does happen, and the staff has referred more depressed people to them since the hanging.

"The better you do the work of recognizing who needs help," I've heard David say at a yawning, uneventful meeting at Charles Street, "the more boring it gets. What we need around here is a good hanging."

"Come on, Rev."

"Not fatal. An attempt. Shake us up."

At the end of the meeting, Jack has a couple of people he wants Lifeliners to see tonight.

"Let's have another cup of coffee first. They'll still be here."

We sit together a while longer, and the men change from talking about other inmates, and start to talk about themselves. They talk about having different personalities in and out of jail.

"I get moody," Tony says. "And that's not like me. Outside, I'm always with people, talking, up to something. In here, I get moody. Into my shell, and don't want to talk to nobody."

"I'm the opposite," Vince says. "At home, if I remember correctly, I'm a pretty sensible, serious kind of guy. In here, I make jokes, put on an act, do silly things I'd never do outside."

"That's a shell too," Joe says, and Jack adds, "Take the officers. Some of them are tough and mean, but they're not like that off the job."

"If you say so." Tony is skeptical.

One of the Samaritans observes that people also put on acts in the other world outside.

"But in here, it's more focused. Every little thing is exaggerated. Sometimes," Joe says glumly through his lush moustache, "I feel like I'm a bug under a microscope."

"There's one thing about Lifeline," Vince says slowly. "When you *are* depressed—O.K., so this is a cliché—it really does help to find that someone feels worse than you. If you weren't part of this team, you wouldn't even know about anyone else's problems. No one in here ever talks about stuff like that. Or if they do, no one listens. They can walk past a cell and see someone hanging. 'None of my business.' They'll walk on by."

"If I wasn't a Lifeliner," Tony says, "I wouldn't have nothing to worry about. After that guy hung it up, I was depressed all night. I couldn't sleep."

"Something you ate."

The serious moment has drifted away. Tony gathers the soup cans. Joe collects the cups and picks up the coffee tray. Jack unlocks the gate and we file along the harshly lit corridor. The men go off somewhere and Ken and I go up the stairs that ring under Jack's high laced boots, and through the guard room. Jack puts us into the trap. The officer on the desk presses the buzzer to let us out, and we go out in the cold to our cars and drive away.

13

"Suicide is the end of one person's unbearable pain, but it's only the beginning of worse pain for the people left behind.

"When Annie killed herself, she killed me too. I was dead for days. I couldn't walk. Then feeling came back, like the blood crowding back in agony when you bring your fingers in from the cold, and that was worse than death. It was true. She'd done it. We'd done it. We'd killed her.

"I blamed myself, her father, her doctor, her friends, this town, her sister—myself, myself, myself.

"And so did other people. Or I thought they did. There was a lot of local publicity. It was what they called a nasty case. I felt I was walking down the street with a scarlet letter on me.

"I had no one to talk to. Duncan was shut up somewhere inside himself. A friend of mine whose son shot himself said, 'You've got about two months. After that, no one wants to hear about it.' Some people don't want to hear about it ever. Duncan and I used to see people crossing the street, or turning their backs in a shop, to avoid us.

"'I feel so badly for them,' Mrs. Stacey said to my sister. 'I mean— to know that it must be their fault.'

"You let go of guilt only for long enough to be angry. Murder's easier. You can be angry with the killer. With suicide—I couldn't say that word for months—you can only be angry with the dead.

"How can you be angry at your dead daughter, you hateful woman? Here comes guilt again.

"Nine months after Annie died, I still needed someone to talk to. Not just anyone. Someone who'd been through it too. I looked for a group of survivors. There wasn't one, so I thought I'd find out how to start one.

"That was my project all that summer. It kept me from going crazy. I went around and talked to all kinds of people and got all kinds of different advice, and believed everything that everybody told me. I went to hospitals, universities, churches, synagogues, therapists who specialized in grief, psychiatrists who specialized in suicide.

"One of them said, 'It's a good idea, but you'll get bored when you get better, and they still need you to stay and help others . . .'

" 'Watch out,' someone said. 'It might prolong your grief.' "

"A doctor said, 'You'll open up a can of worms and not know how to deal with it.' "

"One opportunist who wrote text books wanted to use the group for research."

At the Boston Samaritans, we had talked to so many people who were falling apart after a suicide that we too had been wondering whether you couldn't bring them together to help each other. But how? Who would be experienced enough to make it work?

A young priest called Tom came to see me. He had been running a widows' group, and found that those who had lost someone to suicide did not quite fit. Their anguish was greater and longer, their emotions more intense and more complicated.

Would he be the key to our nebulous idea of a group? Would we be the people to help bring his idea to life?

At the end of that summer, I went to see Tom and his widows. I had to follow up every lead and make notes and compile such a perfect piece of research that actually starting a group would be almost irrelevant.

Tom had just talked to the Samaritans. I was the missing link.

"Let's do it," I said to Beth.

"My research isn't finished."

"Enough. We can do it, Beth. Let's go."

At the first meeting, there were Beth and Duncan and two other couples and Tom, and Sally from the Samaritans. They had no idea how they would run this group or how it would work. They started by going around the table, for everybody to tell why they were here, and something about the suicide.

People started to talk, openly, agonizingly. The others listened, and things were brought out that had never been said before. They thought they were preparing to plan, and then spontaneously this was it. They were doing it. Here it was—the can of worms—and opening it was what this group was all about.

"I never let anyone know I felt like that," one of the mothers said. "I don't think I even let myself know." She sighed. "What a relief. A safe place to talk."

So the group became known as Safe Place. It met every two weeks with Tom and one of the Samaritans, and more and more people with terrible needs came to talk about children, mothers or fathers, husbands or wives, brothers or sisters, friends, sometimes somebody who had been dead ten years or more.

Beth and Duncan got so much strength from Safe Place over the months, that they were able to agree to be part of a television program about teenage suicide.

They did not think it would hurt them, and they thought it might help other people. The more they talked to the attractive, persuasive television people, the more they felt it was their duty. A gift to society. Annie wouldn't mind. It would be a sort of celebration of her.

And it might be—well, not fun, but exciting to be behind the scenes in a studio. If you have never been on television before, it's awfully hard to say no.

But television people must do things their way, if they are going to stay in business. However serious the subject, they have to provide dramatic entertainment, as well as information, if anybody is going to watch. They have to simplify complicated things. To make a cohesive program, they have to make up their minds what line they are taking, and make the material fit.

There are promises of safeguards, privacy, wishes respected. . . . Why do they make these promises? But if they didn't, suffering people wouldn't go on their programs, and suffering people make good television.

The long taping sessions seemed to go all right. Beth felt that she and Duncan had told Annie's tragedy as it was—needless, inexplicable, a mystery never to be understood.

When she saw the tape that had been edited for the show, it seemed like someone else's story. Inevitably, things were cut, or transposed.

"I never said that."

"Yes Beth, you said exactly that."

"But not in that context. I said I was a perfectionist. But about myself. It's all wrong. Important things are left out. Where's Dr. Roberts? Where's Annie's friend?"

"They didn't fit."

"I look ghastly."

"You look great."

She did, in fact, with her marmalade hair cut like a child's, and her steady eyes.

And why—she could not say this aloud, because the wound it had made was so deep—*why did you make it look like my fault?*

It was not obvious. There were no conclusions, nothing written into the script. The reaction of a disinterested observer was probably no more than, "There's those people; their daughter killed herself, and that's so sad."

But Beth, who saw and heard herself on the screen as a selfish perfectionist parent, pressuring a sensitive daughter into achievements, imagines the audience saying, "No wonder she killed herself, with that mother."

Duncan came out of it all right, because he cried in front of the camera, so that made him the hero, the compassionate one.

One of the family pictures of Annie that was shown and fondly cut back to several times, had been taken one Christmas when she was clowning with her brother's harmonica to make him laugh. She sits hunched over, her long blond hair hanging over her knees, her fingers bunched against her mouth. Because you can't see the harmonica, and because of what the commentary implies, it looks as if she were holding herself together in tense misery, biting all her nails.

Mrs. Stacy asked Beth's sister, "How much did they get paid for that?"

Since adolescent suicide became fashionable, there have been so many other similar programs, all wanting real live victims, they are running out of people willing to be interviewed.

I've seen the same rather frowsy girl two or three times on television, talking about her suicide attempts. She is quite smug about it, and increasingly aggressive. You could make a whole career that way.

When Beth's television career was over, she went back to Safe Place and raged a bit, and told the others never to get talked into. . . *never.* . . and felt better.

There are more Safe Place groups now, some of them in Samaritan centers. If one of our volunteers leads the meeting, it is as themselves, not as a Samaritan. We had hoped to be able to help the people who came, but it turns out that they didn't need us. They needed each other.

One woman actively resented us, as in some way allied to the very person who had hurt her so badly. To one of the men, we were an unspoken reproach, as if we were saying, "There is always one more thing that can be done to help a suicidal person to stay alive. Why didn't you do it?"

He objected to one of the posters which said, "SUICIDE DOESN'T HAVE TO HAPPEN."

"Why don't you add, 'so why did you let it?'"

He was a very angry man, rather contentious in the meetings, picking fights with his wife.

"Why didn't you . . . If only you'd called him . . ."

"Look—you said *you'd* call. . . ."

If accusations erupt, the group has a way of absorbing the bitterness. Things that need to be said between families can sometimes be said less painfully in the cushioning safety of outsiders. People don't analyze or criticize, but as the weeks go by, a husband and wife may talk themselves into an understanding of the extent to which the things going wrong in their marriage may have affected their child.

It's better to face this at Safe Place, where it's all right to cry and scream and fall asunder, than alone at home, isolated from each other by grief.

A boy left a suicide note once that said optimistically, "Sometimes something like this helps to bring a family together."

There are more people at the Safe Place meetings than just those around the table. There are the people you never see. You get to know them quite well—the people the others have come to talk about. Invariably they are described as special, beautiful, talented, lovable.

Was there ever a suicide whom nobody cared about? Yet when people are suicidal, they always think, "Nobody cares."

Tom thinks that the meetings are a way of keeping the dead person alive a bit longer. Suicide is so short and fast. The people left behind can't let go of someone they love as quickly as that person has let go of life.

So even guilt can be useful, up to a point. It may be the only thing that still connects you to the dead person, one last thing you can do for them, before you let go.

But there are people who came to Safe Place meetings who didn't let go of a breast-beating guilt that had become narcissistic.

"No one's pain is as great as mine."

They hogged everyone's time, and wouldn't hear another voice, and the group got restless.

Tom had a nice way of saying, "Why don't you just listen now and relax for a bit, Maureen. You've said things that people may want to talk about, and it may help you." But he really meant, "Shut up!"

Same thing if someone started to preach at the others. Once, a worthy woman invited a sobbing mother to "put your hand in the hand of your Lord Jesus Christ, and you'll be all right."

"That might be a little difficult for Rachel," Tom said equably, "since Rachel is Jewish."

The people who are letting go of guilt about the suicide sometimes make a grab backwards at it.

"I had a good day yesterday, and it made me feel awful. How can I feel happy when he's dead?"

Or, "I felt like hell yesterday, but in a way, it felt good, because I ought to feel like hell."

Other people recognize that same absurdity in themselves, and it can be laughed at.

Traveling with the group through guilt and grief, the survivors arrive at the point where they must make a choice. Am I going to die too, along with the person I loved, or am I going to start living again among other people?

"You're doing exactly what my mother did." A young man leaned across the table to a woman who was wallowing. "And, my God, my mother—she might just as well have died with Johnny. She did die, as far as I'm concerned. Is that what you want?"

It's usually a very mixed group. It changes character, as different people come in, or leave, or return with new ideas. But somehow their question for each other emerges always as "So what are you going to do now?"

And the answer, no less powerful even when it is unspoken, is always, "You've got to live."

14

"The Samaritans in *America*? You could never make it work."

Somehow, we have. The quiet tide moves on. Step by step, other people have taken the Samaritans forward and achieved things far beyond my range, and there will be thousands more, who will carry it further.

Although I love to help plan the new branches, I am getting ready now to drop more and more into the background and do what I wanted to do all along—only I had to organize a branch where I could do it: sit by the telephone and have the privilege of sharing someone's life at what may be one of its worst times.

Last night I talked to a woman who called because she was lonely, and then talked about anger and hate, because her husband was not at home, and she knew where he was.

A man wanted to talk about his wayward son . . . but really wanted to talk about himself.

A drunk man kept calling and hanging up after a few words of abuse. He did not want to talk to either me or Max. "I talk only to Jesus."

On the big sofa in the dim light of the main room, a very young girl with a bruised face slept with a week-old baby, waiting for the battered women's shelter people to come and get her in the morning.

Not a special night. No emergencies. Nobody holding onto life by the thread of a telephone line.

Max, who is more patient than I, listened to a woman who has been reciting the same grievances about her neighbors, with seasonal variations, for at least two years. He talked for a long time to a young boy, alone at home, referred to us by the police after they arrested his father.

Henry played his guitar to me over the telephone. A woman called abour four o'clock, to see if someone was here. "I've just woken from a nightmare. This is always my worst time. I'm awake now for the day."

She didn't want to talk. She just wanted to know that someone else was awake.

Toward dawn, old friend Ray called. Sometimes he drinks himself through incoherence to where he sounds sober. In this blackout state, he is often a key figure in world events. Tonight, he had just returned from Israel, where he was someone's bodyguard at a summit conference.

Another night, he had been in one of the helicopters on the Iran rescue mission. He was in Cairo when they shot Anwar Sadat, and in St. Peter's Square on a special mission for the Cardinal when the Pope was shot. Sometimes he is the President's undercover man on Cape Cod. Sometimes his father has left him a million dollars. He is grandiose, but so well informed about details that volunteers who have not talked to him before are afraid they are hearing state secrets.

The young mother was up and washed, with her hair combed back, feeding the baby peacefully on the sofa. After several hours' sleep, she was not so sure she wanted to get away.

"How come it isn't the people you *don't* love who beat up on you?"

She wanted me to call the women's shelter and tell them not to come.

In the telephone room, where the sun was seeping into the empty street outside, Max had had three silent calls. Someone was there. He could hear breathing for a minute, then they hung up.

The fourth time, the caller had evidently said it was the wrong number, and Max knew enough to say, "No—it's not the wrong number. Don't hang up. Tell me what's wrong."

I often think how difficult it would be to make that first call to an unfamiliar number, especially when you are anxious and vulnerable, a crab without its shell.

The Samaritans . . . who are they? Is it a church? A clinic? Will they want my name and address and telephone number before they'll talk to me? Are they sweet old ladies who'll tuck the telephone under their chins so they can keep on knitting, or will they use prefabricated jargon and want me to deal with the issues? Are they ordinary people like me?

What will they think of me, and the stupid mess I've made of my life? It will sound too trivial to take up their time. They must have a lot of people worse off than me.

I imagine myself making that first call. I think about some terrible calamity. Someone I love has died through my fault. I hardly dare invent it on this page. I can't write books any more. Better not say that either, in case of readers' letters: "Well, you can't."

I'm alone. I can't talk to anybody I know. They think I am strong and resilient, because I always have been. I've told them I'm all right, and they believe it. I'm so alone. My dog also died in the car crash. Who can I talk to? Where can I hear a voice at three-thirty in the morning? The police? A telephone operator?

I dial 0 and say I need someone to talk to. I get a number. What will they say? If they're sorry for me, I'll cry. If they're not, I'll know they don't understand. If they put me on hold, I'll hang up. Well, I can hang up anyway. What have I got to lose?

Perhaps I would not ring at all. But I would know that I could. Perhaps we are some small help even to people who may never contact us, by being there, as more alternative.

If things get worse, I could just call those people. . . .

Epilogue

When Monica Dickens died on Christmas day, 1992, newspapers from around the world eulogized her. The *London Times*, for example, claimed that Monica Dickens opened the world "behind the scenes, the world below stairs, and often the squalid world," while *The Daily Telegraph* spoke of her as benevolent, humorous, and of "unmistakable middle class decency."

One paper referred to her as a "dickens of a character," while another said she was the "maid-of-docufiction." *The Independent* of London editorialized: "Charles would have approved of everything about her: her open-mindedness, her fighting spirit, her practical sense. . . ." And a reader of the London *Sunday Express* lauded Monica's books for telling a story straightforwardly, with dexterity and "a great deal of skill." Effusively, these British newspapers went on, praising the considerable talents of Monica Dickens and lamenting her passing.

The first memorial service for Monica Dickens was on January 29, 1993, at St. Mary Abbots in Kensington.

The ceremony opened with Stanford's *Prelude in G*, followed by William Russell's *Voluntary in G*. Monica's cousin by marriage, Audrey Dickens, read an excerpt from *An Open Book*, and British TV personality, Johnny Morris read from Longfellow's *The Song of Hiawatha*. Clare Alexander, publishing director of Viking Books, addressed the audience about Monica's ability to write and, more importantly, how to be a friend.

After several hymns and prayers, P.D. James spoke about the "eccentricity of an upper-class ex-debutante earning her living as a cook and general servant." Monica Dickens, said James, "wrote about what she knew and she wrote with humour, with compassion and with true literary artistry." If James had to choose one word that would describe Monica Dickens, it would be, she said, "warmth." Even Dickens's novels "welcomed" the reader to share her experiences. "She was a popular writer in the best sense of the word, responsive to her readers, wanting to share her vision, her understanding . . . and her life."

Continuing, James said that Monica wrote "about the miseries as well as the joys of life; for she had experienced them." One writer had given the opinion about Monica that she "did not really believe in evil"; thus, "Fagin and Bill Sikes would have been beyond her reach." James said Dickens did believe in evil, "but she believed even more strongly that evil can be overcome by good." When James pondered the subject matter of Monica's books over the years, she could not escape the conclusion that "Charles Dickens would have been . . . very proud of his great-granddaughter."

The next speaker, like P.D. James, was an old friend of Monica's. Sarah Hollis noted that one of Monica's strongest attributes was to make people around her feel important. She said, in remembrance of her friend:

> Thank you, Monica, for all the love and warmth you gave us
> Thank you for all the fun you provided—and the laughs.
> Thanks for teaching us to be brave—positive—and resilient.
> Thank you for all the doors you opened for us.
> And thank you for always being interested, for always caring
>   and making us feel that we really mattered.

Hollis said that even when Dickens was gravely ill, her curiosity and compassion "extended to those who cared for you." Her legacy, Hollis averred, "will never be eroded by time."

Her old friend and mentor Chad Varah spoke at the memorial service about Monica's research on the Samaritans: "She came, she saw, and was conquered." The talent she had as a writer also assured her success as a Samaritan. "Her shrewdness and insight were always humane, and her gentle mockery was without malice."

In the United States, the Associated Press obituary of Monica Dickens ran in 215 newspapers. Some papers, particularly in the New England areas where Monica was best known, wrote their own stories.

The Boston Globe editorialized that Monica would be remembered as a "lively, no-nonsense person who spoke of her work on the edge of death [as a Samaritan] with a sense of both its everyday reality and its eternal mystery."

The *Falmouth Enterprise* editorial remembered 1964, when the Dickens clan gathered at North Falmouth to celebrate the 60th wedding anniversary of her parents, Mr. and Mrs. Henry Charles Dickens. They cut the cake with Charles Dickens's court sword. So many good times. So many memories.

The *Cape Cod Times* joined in eulogizing Monica. "The Samaritans have lost a great friend, but it's unlikely that they ever will lose her inspired example of generosity and caring. This is a time of year [the Christmas season] when we give thanks, and Monica Dickens Stratton's many friends on Cape Cod surely are giving thanks this Christmas week for the privilege of having been a part of her extraordinary life."

"A Celebration and Remembrance honoring the Life of Monica Dickens Stratton" was held in Falmouth on 20 February 1993 at St. Barnabus Memorial Church. The Reverend Robert B. Appleyard, Jr., welcomed the audience, and was followed by a hymn, "For the Beauty of the Earth." Monica's step-granddaughter, Susan Stratton, read excerpts from Monica's *Talking of Horses*, and Monica's son-in-law, Bob Swift, read "On Death."

Her old friend and colleague in the Samaritans, Shirley Karnovsky, addressed the congregation. She spoke at length about the first experiences of the Boston Samaritans at the Arlington Street Church (fully described in *Befriending*). The experiences, Karnovsky related, were "wonderful."

We always had a pot of coffee brewing, [and] street people came in regularly, and in fact slept outside at the entrance to the center, and we had to climb over them when we came in the door. One man came in regularly with his dog which never failed to vomit all over the sofa. Monica was undeterred. She loved the center and no one ever complained about the setup.

Monica never felt rejected by a refusal of financial support, but simply put it aside and went on to the next. She was so energetic and so enthusiastic that it was infectious, and it helped everyone to give their time and more to ensure the first branch of the Samaritans in the United States would be a success.

The obituaries, editorials, and memorial services for Monica were sincere outpourings of affection for a much beloved and admired author and humanitarian. Her influences, to be sure, continue to this very day, as her books are still read and as thousands of Americans each year get in touch with the Samaritans, who are now located in every large city in the country. Monica Dickens's legacy lives on.

CARLTON JACKSON

Sources

Albany Times-Union (NY), 28 Dec. 1992.

The Berkshire Eagle (Mass.), 27 Dec. 1992.

The Boston Globe, 28 Dec. 1992.

Burlington Free Press (Vermont), 28 Dec. 1992.

Mary Calvert, Interview; 18 May 1993.

The Cape Cod Times, 29 Dec. 1992.

Congressional Record, 100 cong. 1 sess (18 Nov. 1987), 176.

The *Daily Mail*, 27 Dec. 1992.

The Daily Telegraph, 28 Dec. 1992.

MSS, Monica Dickens, Noakes Hill; Berkshire, England.

Monica Dickens. *An Open Book*. London: Heinemann, 1978.

Monica Dickens. *The Listeners*. London: Heinemann, 1970.

The Falmouth Enterprise (Mass.), 29 Dec. 1992.

The Guardian, 10 Jan. 1993; 28 Dec. 1992.

Sarah Hollis, Remarks at Memorial for Monica Dickens, 29 Jan. 1993.

The Independent, 31 Dec. 1992.

P.D. James, Remarks at Memorial for Monica Dickens, 29 Jan. 1993.

Shirley Karnovsky, Remarks at Memorial for Monica Dickens, 20 Feb. 1993.

Letters from various present and former Samaritan volunteers who wished to remain anonymous.

The Newbury Weekly News (Berkshire) 31 Dec. 1992.

The New York Times 27 Dec. 1992.

The Sunday Express 27 Dec. 1992.

The Times, London, 28 Dec. 1992.

Chad Varah, Interview, 19 May 1993.

Chad Varah, *The Samaritans*. London: Constable, 1980.

The Washington Post 28 Dec. 1992.

Index

Alberta (Canada), 48
Alcoholics Anonymous, 27, 28
Alexander, Clare, 115
American Psychiatric Association, 79
Appleyard, Rev. Robert B., 117
Arlington Street Unitarian Church, 20, 21, 42, 54, 63, 75, 117
Army Corps of Engineers, 71
Australia, xiii, xxiii, 50, 57, 82

Bahrain, x
Beacon Hill, 15, 41
Befrienders International, x
Belfast, 75
Berkshire Downs, xxv
Boston, xxii, xxiii, 2, 8, 10, 11, 12, 14, 17, 20, 21, 23, 27, 28, 31, 33, 35, 36, 39, 40, 42, 44, 47, 49, 50, 53, 57, 58, 60, 63, 64, 65, 67, 75, 79, 84, 87, 88, 92, 97
Boston Globe, 14, 15, 116
Bourne bridge, xxiii, xxiv, 49, 67, 68, 72, 73
Bridgewater, 29
Brightwalton, xxv
Brimmer Street, 15
Brookline, 61
Burma, xiii

Cairo, 112
Calcutta, 75
Caldwell, Taylor, xviii
California, 48
Calvert, Mary, vii
Cape Cod, xvii, xviii, xxi, xxii, xxiii, xxiv, 4, 9, 29, 40, 47, 48, 49, 50, 56, 63, 64, 67, 68, 71, 73, 112, 117

Cape Cod Times, 116
Charles Street Jail, 97, 98, 99, 102
Closed at Dusk, xxvi
Commons, 20, 84
Commonwealth Avenue, 57
Congressional Record, xxiii
"Country Club," 99

Daily Telegraph, 115
Dear Dr. Lily, xxiv
The Decorated Corpse, xxiv
Denmark Hill, xi
Dickens, Audrey, 115
Dickens, Charles, xiii, xiv, xv, xvi, xvii, xxiii, 13, 115, 116, 117
Dickens, Henry Charles, 117
Dickens, Monica, ix, xi, xii, xiii, xiv, xv, xvi, xvii, xviii, xxv, xxvi, xxvii, 23, 72, 115-18
Dietz, Jean, 14
"dime-droppers," 99
Dunedin Hospital, xxvi
Durkheim, Emile, xiii

"Eighth Principle," xx
Enchantment, xxvi
The End of the Line, xviii, xix, 1
England, xiii, xvii, xxv, xxvi, 7, 8, 12, 20, 73, 76

Fairbanks, Rollin, 8, 9, 11, 20
Falmouth Enterprise, 117
The Fancy, xvi
"the Farm," 99
Finland, xiii
Flowers in the Grass, xvi
Follyfoot series, xxi

119

Gaines, Renford, 20
Gloucester Road station, 4
Golan Heights, xxiii
Golden Gate bridge, 49, 73
Goodwill Industries, 26

Hammersmith, xiv
The Happy Prisoner, vii, xvi
Harrods, xvi
Harvard Square, 8-9
Harvard University, 79
Hertfordshire Express, xvi
"the Hill," 99
Hollis, Sarah, xxvii, 116
Hong Kong, 75
Human Services department (Mass.),
    88, 90, 94

Imara, Mwalimu, 20, 21, 22, 34, 42,
    44
Independent (London), 115
India, xiii
"Instant Jesus," 2
Iran, 112
Ishai, Marvin, xxiii
Israel, 112

James, P.D., 116
Joseph, Michael, xv
Joy and Josephine, xvi

Karnovsky, Shirley, 117
Kensington, xviii, 4, 115
Kübler-Ross, Elizabeth, 20

Last Year When I Was Young, xxi
Land's End Syndrome, 48
Le Suicide, xiii
Lifeline, 89, 90, 91, 92, 93, 94, 97, 98,
    99, 100, 102, 103
The Listeners, xviii, xix
London Times, 115

Mariana, xvi
Martha's Vineyard, 47, 49
Massachusetts General Hospital, 13
Massachusetts Institute of
    Technology, 9
Maudsley Hospital, xi
Miracles of Courage, xxiv
Morris, Johnny, 115
Murphy, Father Kenneth, 11
My Turn to Make the Tea, xvi

Nantucket, 47, 59
New Silver Beach, 51
New Zealand, xiii
Nietzsche, Friedrich, 18
"No Hopers," 50
North Falmouth, xviii, xxi, xxiii, xxiv,
    29, 63, 73

Old Academy, 73
An Open Book, xxi, 115
One of the Family, xxvi
One Pair of Feet, xvi
One Pair of Hands, xv, xvi

Pakistan, xiii
"paper-hangers," 100
Pine Street shelter, 35
Poland, xiii
Priestley, J.B., xvi
Protestant work ethic, 40
Prudential Insurance Company, 42, 44
Public Gardens, 20, 27, 31
Pudding Lane, xxv

Radcliffe University, 79
"the Ranch," 99, 102
Rescue, 11
Rhodesia, xiii
Rummikub, xviii

Sadat, Anwar, 112
Safe Place, 106, 107, 108, 109

Sagamore bridge, xxiii, xxiv, 49, 67, 68, 69, 72

St. Barnabas Church, 63, 64, 117

St. Martin-in-the-Fields, 21

St. Mary Abbots, 115

St. Paul's, x, 3

St. Paul's Girls' School, xiv

St. Stephen Walbrook, ix, x, 1, 4, 11, 21, 64, 75

Salvation Army, 35

Samaritans, x, xi, xii, xiii, xvi, xviii, xix, xx, xxi, xxii, xxiii, xxiv, xxv, 1, 18-31, 32-38, 39-45, 47-62, 63-74, 75-78, 79-85, 87-95, 97-100, 111-13

San Francisco Bay, 49

Scandinavia, xiii

Scarred, xxvi

Scotland, 75

Scrabble, xviii

"Seven Principles of the Samaritans," xii

Shakespeare, William, xvii

Singapore, xiii, 75

Social Security Administration, 25

Sri Lanka, x, 75

Stratton, Pamela, xxi, xxiv, 51

Stratton, Prudence, xxi, xxiv

Stratton, Roy Olin, xvii, xviii, xxi, xxii, 8, 29, 39, 40, 51

Stratton, Susan, 117

Studds, Gary, xxiii

Sunday Express (London), 115

Swift, Bob, 117

Talking of Horses, xxi, 117

Thursday Afternoons, xvi

Tufts University, 79

United Way, xxiv

U.S. Corps of Engineers, xxiii

Varah, Chad, ix, x, xi, xii, xiv, xviii, xix, xx, xxi, xxii, xxv, xxvi, 7, 17, 22, 33, 36, 63, 75, 76, 116

Vietnam War, 21

Viking Books, 115

Voltaire, 1

Walpole State Prison (Mass.), 87, 100

West, Rebecca, xvi

Wiseman, Avery, 13, 76

Woman's Own, xvii

Woods Hole, 49

World's End series, xxi